Walter Robson

Access to **History**

Crown
Parliament
and
People

1 5 0 0 - 1 7 5 0

Oxford University Press

OXFORD
UNIVERSITY PRESS

Great Clarendon Street, Oxford OX2 6DP

Oxford University Press is a department of the University of Oxford.
It furthers the University's objective of excellence in research, scholarship,
and education by publishing worldwide in

Oxford New York

Auckland Cape Town Dar es Salaam Hong Kong Karachi
Kuala Lumpur Madrid Melbourne Mexico City Nairobi
New Delhi Shanghai Taipei Toronto

With offices in

Argentina Austria Brazil Chile Czech Republic France Greece
Guatemala Hungary Italy Japan South Korea Poland Portugal
Singapore Switzerland Thailand Turkey Ukraine Vietnam

Oxford is a registered trade mark of Oxford University Press
in the UK and in certain other countries

Oxford is a registered trade mark of Oxford University Press
in the UK and in certain other countries

ISBN:978 0 198335443
ISBN:0 19 833544X

15 14

Typeset by MS Filmsetting Limited, Frome, Somerset
Printed in Singapore by KHL PRINTING CO PTE LTD

Acknowledgements

Page 4tl British Library, bl E.T. Archive; p5 Bodleian
Library; p6 British Library; p8l National Trust/Upton
House (Bearsted Coll.)/Angelo Hornak, r Mary Evans; p9
Mansell Collection; p1ll Bridgeman/Guildhall Library,
London, r Bridgeman/Ecole des Beaux Arts; p12tl
Bridgeman/Rafael Valls Gallery, London; p13 Mary Evans;
p14bl & p15 National Portrait Gallery, London; p17l & r
Mansell Collection; p18, p19bl & br National Portrait
Gallery; p21cr Mansell Collection; p23t British Museum, b
National Portrait Gallery; p25tr British Museum, c Mansell
Collection, bl E.T. Archive/Victoria & Albert Museum;
p26t National Gallery of Scotland, c Bridgeman/V & A;
p28b Scottish National Portrait Gallery; p30bl Slide File, c
& br British Museum; p31tl & b British Library, tr National
Library of Ireland; p32 Bibliteek van de Rijksuniversiteit te
Gent; p34 National Portrait Gallery; p35 & p36br National
Library of Wales, p37tl Wales Scene, bl Royal Commission
on Ancient & Historial Monuments in Wales; p37t Mary
Evans, b National Library of Wales; p39 Mansell Collection;
p40tl H.M.S.O., b National Portrait Gallery; p41 E.T.; p43
Ashmolean Museum, Oxford; p44l National Portrait Gal-
lery, r Scottish National Portrait Gallery; p45bl National
Portrait Gallery, br Mansell Collection; p46 British
Library; p47 Weidenfeld & Nicolson; p49 Mansell
Collection; p51tl Mary Evans, tr Royal Society; p52 & p55tc
& tr National Portrait Gallery; p56t Oxford City Council/
Thomas Photos, b National Portrait Gallery; p57bl
Bridgeman/Blenheim Palace, Oxfordshire; p58 t & b
National Portrait Gallery; p59 British Library; p60 Edin-
burgh Photographic Library; p62br & p63b E.T.; p64
National Trust/Ron Fox; p66 Hulton Picture Company;
p67cl Mansell, cr Slide File; p68tr Fotomas Index, bl Slide
File; p69 National Maritime Museum; p70bl & p72 Mansell
Collection; p75t, c, b National Portrait Gallery; p76
Museum of London; p77tl E.T., tr Mary Evans; p78tr John
Cleare; p79 Mary Evans; p80 Mansell Collection; p82
British Library; p83 & p84 Mansell Collection; p86tl
Mansell, bl Mary Evans; p87 Michael Holford; p88 Mansell
Collection; p89t & b Chipchase Castle; p90t Michael
Holford, b National Trust; p91t National Trust/R. C.
Wylie, b Nat. Trust/J. Whitaker; p92t Nat. Trust/Rob
Matheson, b. Giraudon/Bridgeman; p93t National Portrait
Gallery, cl Nat. Trust/Ray Hallett, cr Nat. Trust/Mike
Williams; p94 & p95t Mansell Collection.

The illustrations are by Peter Kent and Brian Walker.

Cover: Chairing the member, by Hogarth: Sir John Soane's
Museum.

Contents

Preface

The title of this series is *Access to History*, and accessibility is its keynote – accessibility to National Curriculum History, in terms of both the Programme of Study and the Attainment Target.

The exercises, which refer to the text, sources, and illustrations, are intended to extend factual knowledge, promote comprehension, and develop a range of skills, all consistent with the revised National Curriculum requirements for knowledge, skills and understanding. The "criteria grid" (at the end of the book) shows how the individual exercises relate to these requirements.

It is not expected that pupils will work through the book unaided. Teachers will wish to omit some exercises and amend others. They will probably decide that some exercises which are set for individual work would be tackled more successfully by using a group or class approach, with the teacher him/herself as leader. The book's aim is to provide teachers with a useful set of resources, not to usurp their role.

The exercises with the fill-in blanks may be either photocopied to provide answer sheets and homework assignments or copied out by the pupils and filled in as they go along.

The Village

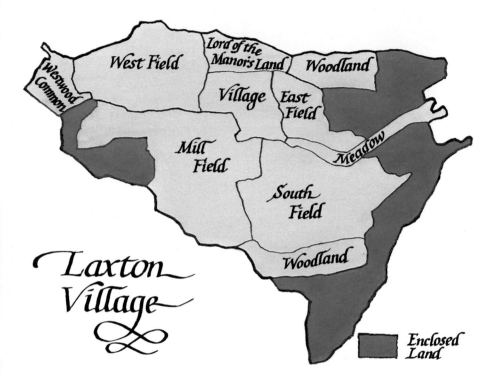

Laxton Village

All the villagers would grow the same crop (e.g. barley) in east field and west field. They would grow another crop (e.g. peas) in south field. Mill field would be left empty (or 'fallow') to let the land rest. Next year, east and west fields would grow peas, south field would be fallow and mill field would grow barley. This is called 'crop rotation'. In Laxton, the same crop was grown in east and west fields.

A farm labourer

A The manor

In the year 1500, nine out of ten English men, women, and children lived in the countryside. They worked on the land. Their homes were in villages or small hamlets. They ate mainly what they grew themselves.

In many places there were still villages with three (or four) **open fields**, divided into **strips**. Most of the villagers had one or two strips in each field, and paid rent for them to the **lord of the manor**. Each year, the peasants grew crops (such as wheat, barley, or beans) in two (or three) of the fields. (Look at **the plan** of **Laxton**.) All the peasants worked together to plough, sow the seed, and reap the harvest. Each man kept the crops which grew on his strips.

As well as the open fields, each manor had some **common** land. The villagers could keep animals there — sheep, cattle, or pigs. Even the poorest peasants could use the common. Most of the animals had to be killed in the autumn, because there was no food for them in the winter. The meat was salted to preserve it, and kept until it was eaten or sold.

You could find villages with open fields all over the Midlands of England. In much of the north and the south-east, the land was divided into smaller fields without strips, and there was no common. These were called **enclosed** villages.

Now try Exercises 1.1 and 1.2.

Exercise 1.1

Read **Section A** and study **the plan**.

Draw a plan of the village of Laxton in 1635. Shade, in different colours if possible:

a The lord of the manor's land,
b The open fields,
c The meadow land,
d The common land,
e Woodland,
f Enclosed land.

Sources

We find out about the past from **sources**. Some of them are **written sources**, such as books. John Leland's account of his travels through England in 1540 (see **Source 1a**) is a good example.

Old coins, maps (such as **Source 1a**), and pictures are also sources. We can learn a lot about the past by visiting churches, old houses, and museums, and studying the **sources** which are kept there.

Source 1a

a *The south and east of Leicestershire is 'champain', and has little wood growing.*
b *From Wakefield to Pontefract (in Yorkshire) is six miles, partly through enclosed land, and partly through 'champain'.*
c *From Wikham to Bishop Waltham (in Hampshire) it is three miles. The land is all enclosed, with good pasture, wood, and corn.*

Three passages from John Leland's account of his journey through England in about 1540. By 'champain' Leland meant open fields.

Source 1b

In villages which have not been enclosed, the poor keep cattle on the common. From the milk, they make cheese and butter, which they sell – the money helps them keep their families. If the common were enclosed, these people would not be able to keep cattle, and would be ruined.

Letter to a Lancashire newspaper, written in 1725.

Source 1c

In the places where the sheep produce the best wool, landlords are not content with rents from their land. They enclose the fields and make pastures. They have houses and whole villages pulled down. The poor farm workers and their families wander about until they have nothing left.

From a book written by Sir Thomas More in 1516.

Harvest time: the Lord of the Manor's reeve keeping an eye on the peasants

Source  **1d**

My father was a yeoman. He paid three or four pounds a year rent to his landlord. He kept a hundred sheep and thirty cows. He was able to afford to send me to school. And when my sisters were married, he gave each of their husbands five pounds. He would always welcome his poor neighbours into his house, feed them, and give them money.

From a sermon preached by Bishop Latimer in 1547.

Exercise 1.2

Examine **Sources 1a, 1b, 1c,** and **1d**.
For each of the sources, find out the answers to these questions:

a What is it?
b Who wrote it or made it? (Write 'Not known' if you do not know.)
c When was it written or made?

Write out your answers in the form of a chart or table.

B Gentry, yeomen, and labourers

The lords of the manor (often called the **gentry**) were the leading men of each district. Everyone looked up to them. All men with money (and their wives) wanted to belong to the gentry. Many a rich merchant from the towns bought land and turned himself into a lord of the manor.

Kings and queens relied on the gentry to keep order and enforce the law. As **Justices of the Peace** (J.P.s), they sat as judges in the local courts, fixed food prices, and collected the taxes that were used to help the poor.

J.P.s got no pay for their work, but they did not complain – they liked being in charge.

The better-off villagers were called **yeomen**. They owned part of their land, and rented the rest from the gentry. Yeomen worked on their own farms, but also employed labourers, and paid them wages. Yeomen made money by selling the corn they grew and the wool from their sheep. Some of them grew rich in the sixteenth century. A few rose to join the ranks of the gentry. (Read **Source 1d**.)

Villagers' wives kept hens and geese. They sold the eggs (and sometimes the birds themselves) at market to make a little extra money.

Below the yeomen were the **tenants** and **labourers**, who owned no land. Tenants rented some land (strips in the open fields) from the lords of the manor, but also earned wages, working for the lords or the yeomen. Labourers had no strips, and worked full-time for wages. Both they and the tenants grew poorer in the sixteenth century.

Now try Exercises 1.3 and 1.4.

Centuries

A **century** is a period of a hundred years.
The **first century** was the hundred years from AD 1 to AD 100.
The **fourth century** was the hundred years from AD 301 to AD 400.
The **tenth century** was the hundred years from AD 901 to AD 1000.
The **fifteenth century** was the hundred years from 1401 to 1500.

Exercise 1.3

Read **Section B** and look again at **Source 1a**. Copy the sentences and write 'True' or 'False' after each one.

a The gentry were the most important people in each district. _____

b All rich people wanted to belong to the gentry. _____

c J.P. stands for Justice of the Peace. _____

d The king paid the J.P.s' wages. _____

e No-one liked being a J.P. _____

f Yeomen owned some land, and rented some. _____

g Yeomen did not have to work in the fields. _____

h At least one bishop was a yeoman's son. _____ (see **Source 1d**.)

i Tenants rented land from the gentry. _____

j Labourers got richer in the sixteenth century. _____

Exercise 1.4

Read the note on 'Centuries.' Now copy the sentences below and fill in the spaces.

a The third century was the _____ years from AD 201 to AD 300.

b The twelfth century was the hundred years from 1101 to _____

c The sixteenth century was the hundred years from _____ to _____

d The _____ century was the hundred years from 1701 to 1800.

e The year 673 was in the _____ century.

f The year 1381 was in the _____ century.

g The year 1620 was in the _____ century.

Draw a time-line, starting at the year 1500 and ending at 1800. Mark the sixteenth, seventeenth and eighteenth centuries.

A J.P. sorts out squabbles with patience and fairness.

Well, you'll just just have to cut it in half, then, won't you?!

C Enclosures

In the sixteenth century, men could become very rich by keeping sheep and selling the wool. Some landowners turned their open fields and commons into pasture for sheep. (Read **Source 1c**.) They put hedges round the new grass fields, so they were called **enclosures**. (The plan of Laxton village shows that in some villages only part of the land was enclosed.)

Enclosures were good for the landowners. But they were not good for the tenants and labourers. They were forced to leave their villages, for they now had no jobs, no land, and no common for their cattle and sheep. Many of them ended up in the towns, as beggars.

Before 1600, men enclosed land to make pasture for sheep. After 1650 there was a change. The population was growing, and the people needed food. So farmers ploughed up the enclosed fields. Some grew wheat, barley, and rye for bread. Others grew clover and turnips, to feed the cattle during the winter. The result was more meat, milk, and butter.

Enclosures cost money. Landowners had to pay for ditches, hedges, and new stock. Very rich **nobles**, who owned big **estates** (more than one manor) could afford the expense. So they enclosed land, and became richer still. But not all gentry could afford to enclose. A lot of them sold their land to the nobles after 1660. And many yeomen sank to the level of labourers.

Now try Exercise 1.5.

Above: Hunting was the favourite sport of the gentry. This picture shows them fox hunting in the eighteenth century.

Above right: Peasant's sport – a village festival with feasting, dancing, and a friendly game of skittles in the sixteenth century

Exercise 1.5

Read **Section C** and **Sources 1a** and **1b** again.
Answer the questions in short paragraphs.

a Which people were in favour of enclosures? Why?
b Which people were against enclosures? Why?
c Had all the villages in England been enclosed,

(i) in 1540? (See **Source 1a**.)
(ii) in 1725? (See **Source 1b**.)

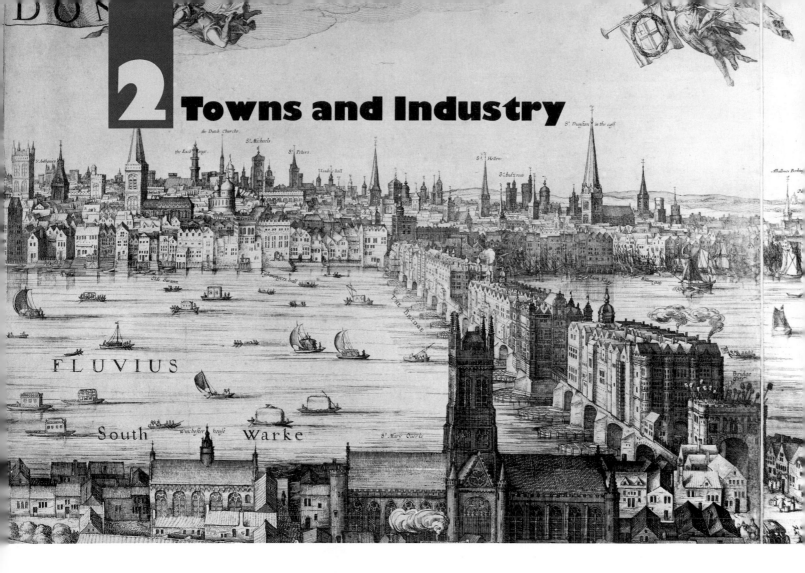

2 Towns and Industry

London in 1616, seen from the south end of London Bridge

A Expanding towns

Only one person in ten lived in a town in England in 1500. The towns were all small. Even London's population was only 50,000. And no other town had more than 20,000 people. Many of England's 700 'market towns' were just big villages.

Things changed between 1500 and 1750. Many thousands of men and women moved from the country to the towns. By 1750, more than 500,000 people lived in London. After 1700, ports such as Bristol and Liverpool, and industrial towns like Birmingham and Leeds grew fast. Even so, no town apart from London had more than 50,000 inhabitants in 1750. The great mass of people still lived in villages or on farms.

All towns were dirty and unhealthy. Houses were packed together in narrow lanes, and families were packed into the houses. (Ten to a room was common.) There were no proper sewers or water supplies. Refuse was thrown into the streets and left to rot. Disease ran riot.

Towns were violent places. The hungry poor easily turned to crime. And since there was no proper police, they often got away with it. Mobs sometimes ran through the streets, looting and burning. Gentlemen in London complained that they were beaten and robbed by drunken roughs outside their own homes.

Now try Exercises 2.1 and 2.2.

TOWNS IN ENGLAND IN 1525

SCOTLAND

Newcastle

York
Hull
Lincoln
Boston Norwich
King's Lynn Yarmouth
Shrewsbury
Coventry Bury St. Edmunds
Worcester Lavenham Ipswich
Hereford Hadleigh
Gloucester Colchester
Bristol Reading LONDON
Salisbury Canterbury
Southampton
Exeter
Totnes

WALES

```
0    50   100  150  200
        Kilometres
```

KEY:
- ■ Population over 50,000
- ■ Population between 10,000 and 20,000
- ⊙ Population between 5,000 and 10,000
- • Population between 3,000 and 5,000

Exercise 2.1

Read **Section A** and study the map. Copy the questions and fill in the blanks.

a After London, which were the three largest towns in England in 1525? _____, _____, and _____

b How many people lived in London, (i) in 1500? _____ and (ii) in 1750? _____

c Which was the largest of these towns in 1525: Hull, Exeter, Hereford? _____

d In which part of England were there most towns in 1525 (north-east, south-east, north-west, south-west)? _____

e In which part of England were there fewest towns in 1525? _____

f Which two ports were growing quickly in the eighteenth century? _____ and _____

g Apart from ports, what other kinds of towns were growing fast in 1750? _____

Source 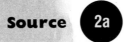 2a

London is a mighty city of business. It is a very busy place, and you can hardly walk along the streets for the crowds. The men and women are well dressed and very proud. They don't like foreigners. They scoff and laugh at them. The boys gather in crowds in the streets and beat them up.

Written by a German visitor to London in 1600.

Source 2b

In every street in London, carts and coaches go thundering past. At every corner, men, women, and children meet in crowds. Hammers are beating in one place, pots clinking in another. There are porters carrying loads, and merchants' men with bags of money. The tradesmen never stand still.

Written by Thomas Dekker, a playwright who lived in London, in 1606.

Exercise 2.2

Read **Sources 2a** and **2b**. Then answer the questions – write one or two sentences about each.

a When were **Sources 2a** and **2b** written?
b Which source was written by an Englishman, and which by a foreigner?
c Both sources say what about London?
d Which things about London are mentioned in **Source 2a**, but not in **Source 2b** – write about two of them.
e Which things are mentioned in **Source 2b**, but not in **Source 2a** – write about two.

B The craftsmen

All towns had weekly **markets**, and villagers would come in on foot to sell butter, cheese, and eggs. They bought what they could not make for themselves, such as cloth, boots, pots and pans. Towns were where these things were made. Skilled **craftsmen** made shoes, hats, barrels, and horses' harness. Dozens of trades were carried on in every town. There were 60 different kinds of tradesmen in Leicester in 1500, and 90 in York.

In the Middle Ages, each trade was organised in a **guild**. The shoemakers' guild said how shoes should be made. They fixed the prices. They made rules about what apprentices had to learn. Craftsmen who did not belong to the guild could not make and sell shoes. And the guild looked after its members – it paid them money when they were ill, and it paid pensions to widows when members died.

Between 1500 and 1750, most of the guilds disappeared. In 1700, fifty towns still had some guilds, but new, go-ahead places like Birmingham had none. Without guilds, tradesmen could make their goods in new ways and use different tools, or even machines.

Now try Exercise 2.3.

A carpenter at work in the Middle Ages

Exercise 2.3

Read **Section B**. Write down this list of tradesmen in a column on the left-hand side of your page:

Baker Butcher Hatter Cooper
Tanner Saddler Goldsmith Lorimer.

Opposite each tradesman, write down what he did, or made. Here are the right answers (but they are in the wrong order!):

made hats   made jewellery and ornaments   made bread
prepared leather   sold meat   made horses' bits
made barrels   made saddles and harness.

A royal charter (agreement) between Richard III and the wax chandlers guild in 1484

C Industry

A weaver

The making of **woollen cloth** was the main industry in England in 1500. (English wool was the best in Europe.) Nearly everyone in England dressed in woollen clothes. England's most important export was cloth. It was sold for high prices in Flanders (modern Belgium).

By 1500 most cloth was no longer made in towns. Country people, working for low wages in their own homes, spun yarn and wove cloth. Rich **clothiers** from the towns sent them the raw wool, collected the woven cloth, and paid their wages.

Between 1550 and 1600 the weavers learned to make a new, lighter kind of cloth, called **worsted**. (They were taught by men from Flanders who settled in eastern England – see **Source 2d**.) The lighter cloth was popular in warm countries, such as Spain and Italy.

Another growing industry was **coal-mining**. In the Middle Ages, wood fires kept houses warm in the winter. But by the sixteenth century there was not enough wood for all the houses in London. Instead, they burned coal, most of which was brought by ship from north-east England.

Experts think that the mines of the north-east produced about 65,000 tons of coal in 1550. By 1690, this had grown to well over a million tons. Londoners wanted more coal, so the mines had to be bigger and deeper on Tyneside. (Most of the coal near the surface had been mined.) Deeper mines meant more danger for the miners – a greater risk of flooding, roof-falls and explosions. (See **Source 2c**.)

Now try Exercises 2.4 and 2.5.

A sixteenth-century mine

Source 2c

A sad accident happened at a pit at Lumley Park (in Durham), not long before we passed through. As the miners were digging out the coal, they came to a hollow place, which may have been part of an old mine. As soon as they broke through into it, there was a great explosion. The force was so great that the earth trembled for miles around. Nearly sixty men lost their lives.

From a book written by Daniel Defoe in 1724.

Causes (or reasons) and Results

A **cause** is a **reason** for something. It is the answer to the question '**Why** did it happen?' or '**Why** was it like that?' e.g. **Why** did so many people move from the countryside to the towns?

Often, there is more than one answer to the question 'Why?' – There are a number of **causes** or **reasons** for most things. Causes come **before** events.

Results come **after** events. For example, one **result** of so many people moving to the towns was overcrowded housing in the towns.

Source **2d**

> *The Flemish workers make kinds of cloth that were never made here before.*
> *Our people copy the foreigners, and make cloth like theirs. The result is more jobs for young people.*
> *The Flemish merchants give jobs to local men and women as well as their own people.*
> *These foreigners live in houses that were empty before, and pay good rents.*
> *The Flemish merchants do a great deal of buying and selling. The extra trade is good for our shopkeepers.*
> *They pay their fair share of taxes and rates.*
> *They work hard, obey the law, live in peace, and in all ways make our city a better place.*

Written in Norwich in 1575, after Flemish workers had been there for about ten years.

Exercise 2.4

Read **Source 2d**.
What were the **results** of the Flemish merchants and cloth-workers coming to Norwich?
Write notes for an essay, using this plan:

a What were the results for the English cloth-workers in Norwich?
b What were the results for the landlords and shopkeepers in Norwich?
c What were the results for all the people of Norwich?

Exercise 2.5

Read **Section C** and the note on 'Causes (or reasons) and Results'.

Answer these questions by choosing sentences from the list marked 'Answers' and writing them down.

a What was the **reason** why English woollen cloth was so good?
b What were two **reasons** why English clothiers were so rich?
c For what **reason** were merchants able to sell English cloth in warmer countries after 1600?
d What was the **reason** why people in London wanted to buy coal?
e What was the **reason** why coal-mines became bigger and deeper?

Answers:
i The coal that lay near the surface had already been mined.
ii English workers learned to make a new, thinner kind of cloth.
iii They paid low wages to the workers and got high prices for the cloth.
iv There was not enough wood for everyone to burn.
v English wool was the best in Europe.

English merchants make a charter with the Flemish

3 Henry VIII

A King and Parliament

In 1509 England's new king was the eighteen-year-old Henry VIII. He was the ruler of Wales as well, and his family, the Tudors, were partly Welsh. But he was not king of Scotland. (Scotland had its own king.)

The king was the real ruler, too. He was the head of the Government. He chose his ministers and advisers, and if he did not like their advice he could ignore it. If they displeased him he could sack them. Unlucky or careless ministers sometimes lost their heads.

The king could declare war and make peace as he liked. Most kings were soldiers, and led their men into battle. But to pay for wars, the king needed taxes. And to charge taxes, or make new laws, the king needed the help of **Parliament**. (Look at the cartoon.)

There were (and still are) two **houses** of Parliament – the **House of Lords** and the **House of Commons**. All nobles (dukes, earls, and barons) and bishops sat in the House of Lords.

Source  3a

A portrait of Henry VIII, painted when he was 45 years old

The KING

The House of Lords

(Lords, landowners and all bishops)

The House of Commons

(Mainly gentry and some rich merchants)

When a bill (a plan for a new Law) is passed by both Houses (the Lords and the Commons) it is sent to the King. If the King gives the Royal Assent (he agrees with it) it will become an Act – a new Law.

The House of Commons contained some of the **gentry** (see Chapter 1), and some rich merchants from the towns.

Parliament did not sit all the time. There was a meeting when the king decided to have one. Usually, this was when he needed money, and wanted new taxes. Between 1509 and 1529, Parliament met only four times, each time for just a few weeks. (After 1529 it met much more often.)

Now try Exercises 3.1 and 3.2.

Exercise 3.1

Read **Section A**, and study the diagram on page 14.
Copy the diagram (with or without the cartoon drawings).
Then add notes answering these questions:

a Parliament had the power to do which two things?
b Who decided when there should be a meeting of Parliament?
c How often did Parliament meet?
d Who were the members of the House of Lords?
e Who were the members of the House of Commons?
f What is a bill?
g What is the 'Royal Assent'?
h What is an Act of Parliament?

Source  3b

I am accused of breaking the law made by Parliament. But I say that this law goes against God's law and the law of the Church. Therefore, I must not obey it. No-one can change God's law, and only the Pope can change the Church's law.

Words spoken in 1534 by Sir Thomas More, who had been Henry VIII's chief minister.

Source 3c

Parliament can abolish old laws and make new ones. It can change the Church. It can make new taxes. It can change men's rights. It can pardon some men, and it can condemn others. Whatever Parliament passes, all must obey.

Written by Sir Thomas Smith in 1565.

Exercise 3.2

Sometimes the sources do not agree with each other. Men and women in the past, just like people today, did not always have the same ideas. It helps us understand the events, and the people who made them, if we look at what they disagreed about.
Read **Sources 3b** and **3c**, then answer the questions.

a Who wrote **Source 3b**, and when did he write it?
b Who wrote **Source 3c**, and when did he write it?
c **Source 3b** says that there are two other kinds of law, apart from the laws made by Parliament. What are they?
d According to **Source 3b**, who is the only person who can change the Church's law?
e **Source 3c** says that Parliament can do what?
f Does the author of **Source 3c** agree or disagree with the author of **Source 3b**? (Write two or three sentences explaining your answer.)

Thomas More

B A son and heir

Henry VIII was clever, handsome, strong, and good at all sports. But he was also selfish, and he could be cruel. He showed his cruelty, above all, in the way he treated his wives.

Like most men in his days, Henry VIII thought that ruling England was a man's job. So he wanted a son to take over when he died. By 1527, though, his only child was a daughter (Mary). (Look at the cartoon opposite.) He, therefore, decided to divorce Catherine, his first wife, and marry again. He hoped that a new wife would give him a son.

As England was still a **Catholic** country, Henry needed the **Pope's** permission for a divorce. The Pope said 'No'. Henry then said that he, not the Pope, was head of the Church in England. He got **Thomas Cranmer**, the Archbishop of Canterbury, to say that he was free to marry again.

Henry did marry again, but his second queen, **Anne Boleyn**, also gave birth to a daughter. A third marriage, to **Jane Seymour**, led at last to the birth of a son, but Queen Jane died in childbirth. Three more wives followed, but no more children.

Now try Exercise 3.3.

Catherine of Aragon was a Spanish princess. She married Henry VIII in 1509. They had six children, but only one of them survived – a daughter called Mary. Mary was born in 1516. Henry divorced Catherine of Aragon in 1533.

Henry VIII married **Anne Boleyn** in 1533. She gave birth to a daughter (Elizabeth) later in the same year. Anne had a son also, but he died at birth. Henry accused Anne of being unfaithful, and had her beheaded in 1536.

Jane Seymour married Henry in 1536. A son (Edward) was born in the next year. Jane died a few days after her son was born.

Henry married **Anne of Cleves**, a German princess, in 1540. Thomas Cromwell, Henry's chief minister, arranged the marriage. Henry had not seen Anne until she arrived in England. When he did see her, he thought she was too plain, and divorced her straight away. Cromwell got the blame, and lost his head.

Catherine Howard was a girl of 19 when Henry married her in 1540. By then, he was middle-aged, fat, and ugly (see **Source 3a**). Catherine was unfaithful, and Henry had her beheaded in 1542.

Catherine Parr was a widow of 31 when she married Henry in 1543. She looked after him and his younger children in the last years of his life. Henry died in 1547, and Catherine died in 1548.

Exercise 3.3

Read **Section B** and study the cartoon above.

Write out these events in the right order (earliest first).
Put the correct date next to each event.

Henry married Anne of Cleves.   Catherine Parr died.
Henry's daughter Elizabeth was born.   Anne Boleyn was executed.
Henry VIII died.   Henry's daughter Mary was born.
Prince Edward was born.   Catherine Howard was executed.
Henry married Catherine of Aragon.

C The English Reformation

A lot of men and women thought there were things wrong in the Catholic Church. Some of them became **Protestants**, or reformers. Protestants were against the Pope. They were against rich bishops living in grand palaces. They thought that priests should pray in their own language, not Latin. They said that priests should be allowed to marry.

The Protestants were pleased when Henry VIII got Parliament to pass laws ending the power of the Pope. The laws said that the king was the head of the Church in England. Bishops had to swear to be loyal to him, not to the Pope. These changes were the start of the English **Reformation**.

Henry VIII was not a Protestant. (He did not want to change the Church service, and he did not want priests to marry.) But he allowed Thomas Cranmer to translate some prayers into English. And he agreed that there should be a copy of the Bible in English in every church.

The idea of closing the monasteries came from Thomas Cromwell, Henry's chief minister. His reason was that the monasteries had masses of silver and jewels, and great estates of land. If the king closed them down, he could take all that they owned. Like all kings, Henry was always short of money.

By 1539 the monasteries and nunneries were closed. The monks and nuns had to leave. The buildings either became parish churches or private houses, or they were left to fall down. The king sold most of the land, silver, and jewels. Then he wasted the money on a useless war.

Now try Exercises 3.4 and 3.5.

A cartoon from a Protestant book published in 1563. It shows Henry VIII trampling on the Pope.

Thomas Cromwell

Exercise 3.4

Read **Section C**. Copy the sentences below and use the answers to complete them.

a Protestants did not think that _____

b Parliament passed an act which said that_____

c Henry VIII did not think that _____

d Thomas Cranmer was the _____

e Henry VIII said that every church _____

f Thomas Cromwell suggested that _____

g Henry agreed with Cromwell's idea _____

Answers:
- priests should be allowed to marry.
- should contain a Bible in English.
- because he wanted the monasteries' land and wealth for himself.
- Archbishop of Canterbury.
- the king was head of the Church of England.
- Henry should close down the monasteries.
- the Pope should be head of the Church.

Source **3d**

The king is the most handsome prince I ever saw. He is above average height. His complexion is fair and bright. He has short auburn hair, combed straight. He has a round face, so beautiful that it would suit a pretty woman. He speaks French and Latin, and some Italian. He plays the lute and harpsichord well. He draws the bow with greater strength than any man in England, and is marvellous at jousting.

Written by an Italian visitor to England in 1515.

Source **3e**

A portrait of Henry VIII painted when he was 29 years old

Fact and Opinion

A **fact** is something which is, or was, true. It is a fact that Anne Boleyn was beheaded.

An **opinion** is what someone thinks, or thought. Henry VIII's opinion was that Anne of Cleves was very plain.

Exercise 3.5

Read **Source 3d** and look at **Source 3e**. Read the note 'Fact and Opinion'.

a Write down two **facts** about Henry's appearance that are mentioned in **Source 3d**.

b What was the Italian visitor's **opinion** of the king's appearance?

c Was the king good at languages? Write down a **fact**.

d Was the king good at music? Write down the Italian visitor's **opinion**.

e Write down a **fact** which shows that Henry was strong.

f Look at **Source 3e**. Do you agree with the Italian visitor's description of Henry VIII? Do you agree with his opinions? (Write a paragraph.)

4 Queen Elizabeth I

A Henry VIII's children

When Henry VIII died in 1547, his only son became **King Edward VI**. But Edward was too young to rule. So England was governed by **Protectors** — first Edward's uncle, the Duke of Somerset, then the Duke of Northumberland.

Both dukes were Protestants, and keen on Church reform. They said that priests could marry. They made people use a new English prayer book. And they got rid of some of the statues and pictures from the churches.

Edward was always a sickly boy, and he died at the age of fifteen. His half-sister **Mary Tudor** then became queen. Mary was a keen Catholic. She brought back the Catholic mass, and said the Pope was in charge of the Church in England again. Many Pro-

testants fled abroad. About 300 who stayed were burned to death by Mary. One of them was Thomas Cranmer.

Burning the Protestants was unpopular. Mary's marriage to King Philip II of Spain was worse. Philip and his Spanish courtiers, who looked down on the English, were hated.

Mary died in 1558, and Henry VIII's other daughter, **Elizabeth**, came to the throne. She was twenty-five years old, unmarried, and alone. Most men (and women) said that she needed a husband to guide her. But who would the husband be? No-one wanted Philip of Spain, or any foreign king. And if the queen married an English lord, all the others would be jealous. Elizabeth's answer was not to marry at all.

Now try Exercise 4.1.

Below right: Edward VI and his Protectors continue Protestant reform

Below left: The Catholic Mary Tudor as a young woman

KING HENRY VIII AND HIS CHILDREN

HENRY VIII king 1509-1547

1st marriage to — Catherine of Aragon

— 2nd marriage to — Anne Boleyn

— 3rd marriage to Jane Seymour

MARY
born 1516
died 1558
Queen 1553-1558

married Philip II of Spain (no children)

ELIZABETH
born 1533
died 1603
Queen 1558-1603

EDWARD
born 1537
died 1553
King 1547-1553

Exercise 4.1.

Read **Section A** and study the family tree, then answer the questions.

a For how long was Henry VIII king?
b How old was Mary Tudor when she became queen?
c For how long was Elizabeth queen?
d How old was Elizabeth when her father died?
e For how long was Edward VI king?

Draw a time-line from 1509 to 1603, showing England's kings and queens.

B Catholics and Puritans

The first of Elizabeth's problems was religion. The Protestants who had fled from Mary streamed back, hoping for support from the new queen. By and large, they were satisfied. Elizabeth said that she, not the Pope, was head of the Church of England. The service would be read from an English prayer book, not sung in Latin. Priests were to be free to marry.

Some English people stayed Catholic, and worshipped in secret. Priests moved by night from house to house, hiding in lofts or in holes between walls. A few Catholics plotted to kill Elizabeth and put her cousin, **Mary Queen of Scots**, on the throne. (See Chapter 5.) They got support from the Pope, who said that Elizabeth had no right to be queen. Priests and plotters who were caught were killed.

Europe's leading Catholic king was Philip of Spain. When Elizabeth had Mary Queen of Scots put to death in 1587, he went to war. He tried, with his **Armada**, to invade England in 1588, but failed. England and Spain were at war for the next sixteen years.

Puritans were also against the Church of England. They said it was just like the Catholic Church, with priests dressed in special robes. They did not like having the service read from a prayer book. Puritans wanted plain churches and services in plain English. They thought the minister should preach a sermon, not read prayers from a book. Elizabeth disliked the Puritans. In the last years of her reign, many of them were thrown into prison, and some were put to death.

Now try Exercises 4.2 and 4.3.

Exercise 4.2

Read **Section B**, then copy the chart and fill in the blank spaces.

	Catholic Church	Church of England	Puritans
Who was head of the Church?			Queen
Did they use a prayer book?	Yes		
The Church service was in which language?			
Could priests (or ministers) marry?			Yes
Did the priests wear special robes?	Yes		

An English galleon from the time of the Spanish Armada

THE TUDOR SEE-SAW

Henry VIII started his reign as a good _____

Henry VIII ended the _____'s power in England, but he was not a Protestant

In _____ VI's reign England became a Protestant country

_____ Tudor was a keen Catholic

Elizabeth made England _____ again

Exercise 4.3

Copy the five drawings of the Tudors on the see-saw. (Draw pin-men and pin-women if you wish.) Copy the captions, and fill in the blank spaces, using words from this list:

Edward   Protestant   Mary
Pope   Catholic

C A woman fit to rule

Henry VIII thought that a woman would not be able to rule England. Elizabeth proved him wrong. There was no doubt that she was in charge of the Government. She chose her ministers, and they obeyed her orders. She listened to her council of advisers, then made up her own mind.

The **court** was where the queen was at any time. It might be in one of her palaces, or it might be in the house of a great lord, when the queen was on tour. She, and all around her, put on a great show. They dressed in fine clothes and jewels, and took part in grand pageants and banquets. All this display was meant to let men know that the ruler of England was a rich and mighty queen, so they should treat her with respect.

Parliament met every three or four years, mainly when the queen needed taxes. And when it met, the Commons were always anxious for the queen's safety. They asked her to marry. They urged her to make stricter laws against the Catholics. They begged her to get rid of Mary Queen of Scots.

Elizabeth had more than one quarrel with the Puritan gentry in the Commons. The Puritans dared to attack the Church of England. She told them that the Church was her affair, not theirs. They replied that the Commons had a right to free speech – they could talk about the Church if they wished. But in the end, the Puritans gave in. Like other Englishmen, they were devoted to their queen.

Now try Exercises 4.4, and 4.5.

Source 4a

We are supposed to have freedom to say what we wish in this House. We need that freedom so that we can advise and warn the queen. But sometimes she does not like what we say. Once she sent us a message saying that we must not talk about religion. Later, she refused to agree to the laws we passed. This pleased the Catholics and traitors, and made them laugh at us.

From a speech made by Peter Wentworth in the House of Commons in 1576.

Source 4b

The queen told me to remind you that she is head of the Church of England. She has the power to put right anything that is wrong in the Church. And she will correct its faults, if it has any. She has told you not to meddle with matters of religion, but you have not obeyed her. She is sorry to have to say these things, for she knows that you are her loyal subjects. But she must warn you not to discuss religion again.

Report by the Speaker to the House of Commons in 1585. He had just had a meeting with the queen.

Source 4c

(The House of Commons) wanted to give the queen advice on the problem of whether she should marry or not, on who should take the throne when she died, and on what to do with Mary Queen of Scots. Most of all, they wanted the 'freedom of speech' to discuss these matters openly.

From a book written by Haydn Middleton in 1987.

Source **4d**

A drawing of Queen Elizabeth I made by Frederico Zuccaro in 1575, when the Queen was 42 years old

Source **4e**

A portrait of Queen Elizabeth I, painted in 1590, when she was 57 years old. Artist unknown.

Primary and Secondary Sources

Letters, diaries, and books written by people who were present, and saw the things they wrote about, are called **primary sources**.

Papers and books written by people who were **not** present are called **secondary sources**. The authors of **secondary sources** must have heard about the events from someone else, or read about them in books. Books that were written hundreds of years after the events they describe, therefore, are **secondary sources**.

Exercise 4.4

Read **Section C** and **Sources 4a**, **4b**, and **4c**. Then read the note on 'Primary and Secondary Sources'.
Write out the sentences, filling in the missing words.

a **Source 4a** is part of a speech made by _____ _____ in 1576.

b The speech in **Source 4a** was made in the _____ of _____ during Queen Elizabeth I's reign.

c **Source 4a** is a _____ source.

d The words in **Source 4b** were spoken by the _____ to the House of Commons in 1585.

e The Speaker (**Source 4b**) had just had a meeting with the _____

f **Source 4b** is a _____ source.

g **Source 4c** was written by _____ _____ in _____

h **Source 4c** was written _____ years after Queen Elizabeth I died. (She died in 1603.)

i **Source 4c** is a _____ source.

Exercise 4.5

Look at **Sources 4d** and **4e**. Discuss the questions in a group, then either write out your answers in paragraphs, or make a tape giving the group's answers.

a Who were the artists, and when did they make their pictures?

b In what ways are the two pictures **i** similar, **ii** different?

c Can you think of any reasons for differences between the pictures?

d Did the artists actually see Queen Elizabeth I?

e Should we believe what the pictures tell us about the queen's appearance?

5 Scotland in the Sixteenth Century

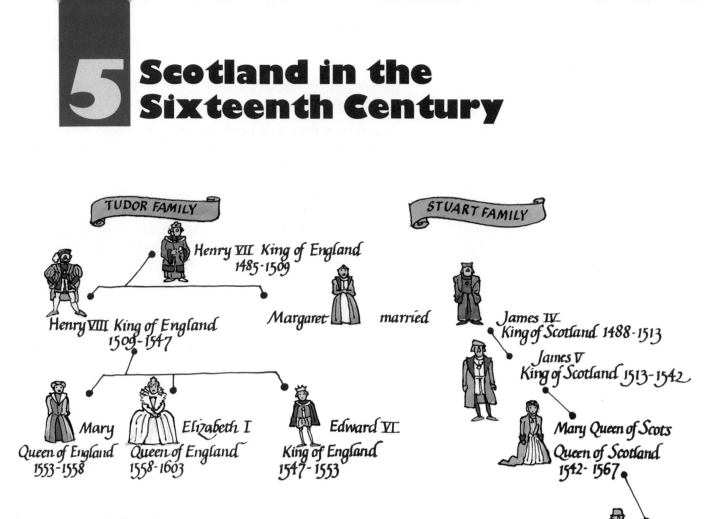

TUDOR FAMILY

Henry VII King of England 1485-1509

Henry VIII King of England 1509-1547

Margaret married

Mary Queen of England 1553-1558

Elizabeth I Queen of England 1558-1603

Edward VI King of England 1547-1553

STUART FAMILY

James IV King of Scotland 1488-1513

James V King of Scotland 1513-1542

Mary Queen of Scots Queen of Scotland 1542-1567

James VI King of Scotland 1567-1625 (King James I of England 1603-1625)

A Proud but poor

Scotland was a proud country, but poor. Its soldiers had fought for, and won, their freedom from England. Scotland had its own king, laws, and army. But the people were mainly peasants. Their food was porridge and oatcakes – from the barley and oats that they grew. They sold the hides of their cattle and the wool from their sheep to pay the rent. Their homes were rough shacks, with earth or stone walls and turf roofs.

Scotland's kings spent a lot of their time at war, either with the English or with their own subjects. The wildest of these were the clan chiefs of the **Highlands** in the north. They stole each other's cattle, fought local wars, and cared nothing for the king. But the earls and lords of the **Lowlands** were not much better, with their plots and civil wars.

Better times came with King **James IV**. James was only fifteen when he became king in 1488. He was a bright young man, quick to learn, full of energy, and well liked. Within a year, he beat the rebel lords in battle, and brought order to the Lowlands. Trade increased, and the towns began to grow. Peace with England was settled when James married an English princess (Henry VIII's sister Margaret).

Then in 1513 James IV foolishly joined the side of France (Scotland's old ally) in a war with England. The Scots were crushed at the Battle of **Flodden**, where James and thousands of his men were killed. His son, King James V, was less than two years old. Scotland sank back into quarrels and civil war between groups of lords, all wanting power for themselves.

B Queen of Scotland and France

In December 1542, James V died, aged 30. The crown of Scotland passed to his daughter, Mary, less than a week old. (We call her **Mary Queen of Scots**.) While Mary was a child, her mother, who was French, governed in her place. When Mary was five, her mother sent her to France, to learn to speak French and behave like a lady of the French court.

At the age of fifteen, Mary married a French prince called **Francis**. A year later, he became king of France – so Mary was now queen of Scotland and France. But in less than two years, she was a widow. And in August 1561, still not nineteen years old, Mary sailed home to Scotland. It was a cold, foreign land that she hardly knew.

When Mary left for France, Scotland was a Catholic country. When she returned, it was Protestant. A preacher called John Knox was now the leading man in Edinburgh. He stirred up the mobs to break the statues in Catholic churches, and burn the pictures. The Scots Parliament passed acts ending the power of the Pope, and banning the Catholic mass. Mary was a Catholic all her life, but could do nothing to save her Church.

Now try Exercise 5.1.

George Wishart, one of Scotland's first Protestants, who was burned to death in 1546. He became a Protestant martyr.

Source 5a

Mary Queen of Scots, aged 16 – A painting made by François Clouet, who lived from about 1520 to 1572. He worked at the French court in the 1550s.

John Knox

Exercise 5.1

Read **Section B**. Draw a time-chart of the early life of Mary Queen of Scots (from 1542 to 1562). Mark the following on the chart:

a Mary was born and became queen of Scotland.
b Mary was sent to France.
c Mary married her first husband.
d Mary's first husband became king of France.
e Mary's first husband died.
f Mary returned to Scotland.

Shade in two different colours the time Mary spent in Scotland, and the time she spent in France.

C Mary's adventures

In July 1565, Mary married **Lord Darnley**, her handsome but foolish cousin. Mary soon found out that he could be jealous and cruel. Darnley hated **David Rizzio**, Mary's secretary, and one night in March 1566, he killed him. Darnley led a gang of thugs into the room where Mary, her ladies-in-waiting, and Rizzio were sitting. The thugs dragged Rizzio out, and stabbed him to death, just outside the door. Mary never forgave Darnley.

A year later, Darnley himself was murdered. The house where he was staying in Edinburgh was blown up in the middle of the night. His body was found outside – he had been strangled. It was said that the **Earl of Bothwell** had killed Darnley. Some people thought that Mary was involved.

Three months after the murder, Mary married the chief suspect, the Earl of Bothwell. This made the Scots think that she was guilty. They rose in revolt, seized her, and put her in prison. But she soon escaped. She fled to England, and begged her cousin **Queen Elizabeth** to protect her.

If Elizabeth had sent Mary back to Scotland, the Scots would have killed her. Instead, she kept her in prison for nineteen years. During that time, some English Catholics plotted to murder Elizabeth, and put Mary on the throne. In the end, Mary was charged with taking part in one of the plots. She was found guilty, and beheaded.

When the Scots rebelled against Mary, they made her year-old son king as **James VI**. The new king was brought up by strict Protestants, who had no time for fun. Meanwhile, the lords and clan chiefs ignored the law and fought their private wars.

Now try Exercises 5.2, 5.3, and 5.4.

The murder of David Rizzio. This picture was painted by Sir William Allan in 1833.

Source **5b**

Mary Queen of Scots, aged about 35, when she was a prisoner in England. This miniature (small portrait) was painted by Nicholas Hilliard, who lived from 1547 to 1619. It was probably painted from life.

Exercise 5.2

Read **Section C**, and study **Sources 5a** and **5b**.
Answer questions **a** to **f** in sentences, and question **g** in a paragraph.

a Who painted **Source 5a**, and when did he live?
b When was **Source 5a** painted? Where was Mary when it was painted?
c Could the artist have painted **Source 5a** from life? Is it a primary or a secondary source?
d Who painted **Source 5b**, and when did he live?
e When was **Source 5b** painted? Where was Mary when it was painted?
f Did the artist paint **Source 5b** from life? Is it a primary or a secondary source?
g What differences between the two portraits can you see? Can you think of any reasons for the differences?

Source **5c**

I know for certain that the Queen regrets her marriage. She hates the King (Darnley) and all his family. David Rizzio, with the consent of the King, will get his throat cut within the next ten days.

From a letter written by the English ambassador in Scotland, three weeks before Rizzio's murder.

Source  **5d**

No more tears now. I will think about revenge.

Words spoken by Mary Queen of Scots soon after the murder of Rizzio.

Source  **5e**

It breaks her heart to think that he (Darnley) is her husband. She cannot think how to be rid of him.

From a letter written by William Maitland, one of Mary's ministers.

Source **5f**

The King's (Darnley's) death is planned. If I do not kill him, I cannot live in Scotland. He will destroy me.

John Hay's account of what the Earl of Bothwell said to him in 1566.

Source **5g**

You and I are the most faithful couple that were ever united. Cursed be this fellow (Darnley) that troubles me so much.

From a letter which Mary was supposed to have written in 1567 to the Earl of Bothwell. Some historians think that it is a forgery.

Evidence

The student of history is like a judge in court. He looks carefully at the pieces of evidence (or sources) left by the people of the past. He asks questions about each source, including: Who wrote or said it and when? Can I believe what this source says? What does it prove?

Exercise 5.3

Read **Section C** again, and read **Sources 5c**, **5d**, **5e**, **5f**, and **5g**. Now it is your turn to be the judge in 'The case of the Darnley murder'. There are five pairs of sentences below. From each pair, choose the one you think is true, and write it out.

a i **Source 5c** proves that Mary was happy before the murder of Rizzio.

 ii **Source 5c** proves that Mary hated Darnley before Rizzio's murder.

b i **Sources 5d** and **5e** prove that Mary planned to kill Darnley.

 ii **Sources 5d** and **5e** only prove that Mary wanted to be rid of Darnley. She was probably thinking of divorce.

c i **Source 5f** proves that Bothwell planned to kill Darnley.

 ii **Source 5f** proves that Bothwell knew about the plan to kill Darnley.

d i **Source 5g** proves that Mary knew about the plot to kill Darnley

 ii **Source 5g** may be a forgery, so it proves nothing.

e i By marrying Bothwell, Mary proved that she had been involved in the murder plot.

 ii Her marriage to Bothwell only proves that Mary was foolish.

The execution of Mary Queen of Scots

Exercise 5.4

Elizabeth was very unhappy about sending Mary to her death. There were reasons for and against it. Here are some of them:

Reasons for having Mary executed:
a Mary was guilty of taking part in plots to kill Elizabeth.
b The Catholics would stop plotting against Elizabeth if Mary was dead.
c Most of Elizabeth's Council and Parliament wanted Mary killed.

Reasons against having Mary executed:
a Mary was Elizabeth's cousin.
b Mary was a queen, and killing a king or queen is a terrible crime.
c Killing Mary might make the Catholics hate Elizabeth even more.
d The kings of France and Spain might go to war to punish Elizabeth.

What would **you** have done if you had been in Elizabeth's position? Discuss what you think with others in a group. One member of the group could tell the class what you think, or you could make a group tape.

6 Ireland in the Sixteenth Century

A Irish and English

England's kings said that Ireland belonged to them. But Ireland's real rulers were its earls and lords. They owned the land, and kept some kind of order among the peasants. Each lord had his castle and his own army. The English ruled only **the Pale**, a small district around Dublin. (Look at the map.)

The lords and peasants were Irish, not English. They had their own language and laws, their own poetry and music. The English, to them, were foreigners. The lords were **vassals** (subjects) of the English king, but that did not mean much to them.

Some English kings tried to take control of Ireland. **Henry VII** knew that rebels might land there, and use Ireland as a base to attack England. So he got **Sir Edward Poynings**, his governor of Ireland, to put Englishmen in charge of all the main castles. And Poynings said that the Irish Parliament could debate no bill that the king of England had not approved.

But to control Ireland, the English had to keep an army there. And that cost money, which few kings could afford. **Henry VIII**, in the first part of his reign, used the old, cheaper ways. He made the Irish lords swear to be loyal, then left them alone. The Irish paid some taxes to Henry, but he did not try to make them obey English laws.

Now try Exercise 6.1.

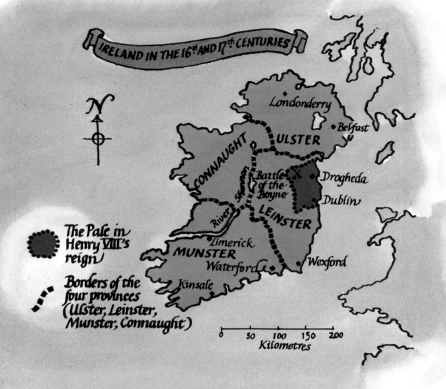

Exercise 6.1

Read **Section A**, and study the map. Write down the answers to the questions. Choose your answers from the list below.

> Waterford Connaught the king of England's judges Munster Limerick the Pale foreigners Drogheda Leinster the governor of Ireland's soldiers Ulster Dublin vassals

a Which was the only part of Ireland that the English really ruled?
b Irish lords and peasants thought of the English as what?
c Poynings said that the Irish Parliament needed whose permission before it debated a bill?
d The English could control Ireland only if they kept what there?
e The north of Ireland is in which province?
f Which two towns were inside the Pale?
g Which town is at the mouth of the River Shannon?
h The south-west of Ireland is in which province?

B King of Ireland

Peace in Ireland never lasted long. In 1534 the Earl of Kildare, the leading Irish lord, was in London as a guest of Henry VIII. Soon a rumour spread in Ireland that Kildare had been killed. The Irish rose in revolt. They were led by **'Silken Thomas'** Fitzgerald, Kildare's son. Henry sent troops, crushed the revolt, and had Silken Thomas put to death.

Henry thought that Ireland needed a firm hand. He made the Irish Parliament pass an act saying that he was **King of Ireland**. (Before then, English kings had been 'Lords of Ireland'.) Another act said that all the land in Ireland belonged to him. The Irish earls and lords had to give him their land. Then he gave it back **on condition that they obeyed him**.

Henry also said that he was head of the Church in Ireland, as he was in England (see Chapter 3). And he closed down the monasteries in the Pale. When he did these things in England, the Protestants were pleased. But there were hardly any Protestants in Ireland – the lords and peasants remained Catholic. To them, the Pope was still the head of the Church.

From this point on, there were **two** main reasons why the Irish did not like the English. The first was the same as before – the English were foreigners. (They did not understand Irish law or history, or the Irish language.) The second was new – the English were Protestants, and the Irish were Catholics.

Now try Exercise 6.2.

Source **6a**

Source 6b

Mellifont Abbey, one of the Irish monasteries closed down by Henry VIII

This shows both sides of an Irish coin issued by Henry VIII. One side (left) shows Henry's name and coat of arms. The other side (right) has the Irish harp stamped in the centre, with the letters 'H.R.' on either side. This stands for 'Henricus Rex' – i.e. King Henry of Ireland.

Source  6c

Irish brigands burning villagers' homes and stealing their cattle. (From a book printed in 1581.)

Source 6d

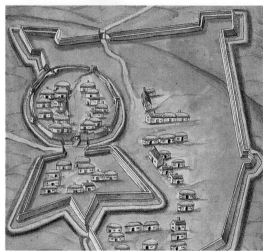

Mount Norris in Armagh – one of the forts the English built to help keep law and order in Ireland

Exercise 6.2

Read **Section B**, and look at **Sources 6a, 6b, 6c,** and **6d**.
On the left side of the page below, you will see the **first halves** of seven sentences about Ireland. On the right side are the **second halves**, but in a different order. Put the correct halves together, and write out the complete sentences.

First half
a Source 6a shows an Irish monastery that was...
b On one side (above) of the coin in **Source 6b**...
c The other side (below) of the coin in **Source 6b** proves that...
d **Source 6c** shows that Irish brigands...
e **Source 6c** shows that Irish villagers were...
f **Source 6c** shows why...
g The fort in **Source 6d** had...

Second half
- the fort in **Source 6d** was needed.
- Henry VIII claimed to be King of Ireland.
- a ditch and a stockade, but not high stone walls.
- closed down by Henry VIII.
- Henry VIII's name and coat of arms can be seen.
- came out of the woods to destroy and steal.
- not able to defend themselves against the brigands.

An Irish chief surrenders to the English governor in the time of Queen Elizabeth

C Elizabeth and Ireland

Soon after Henry VIII's death, the Irish found a **third** reason to hate the English. Queen Mary Tudor began the **plantations**. English troops pressed west from the Pale, drove out the Irish lords and peasants, and gave their land to English settlers – English farmers were 'planted' on Irish land.

Queen Elizabeth I tried more plantations, further to the west and north. But plantations led to revolt – angry Irishmen attacked the settlers. Lords (such as the **Earl of Desmond** in Munster) and their peasants were ready to fight for their laws, their Church, and their land. English troops crushed the revolts. They killed the rebels, and burned their crops and homes.

The most serious Irish revolt began in Ulster in the 1590s. It was led by **Hugh O'Neill**, Earl of Tyrone. He called on all Irishmen to fight for the Catholic Church and an Ireland free from English rule. The lords and peasants of Ulster and Munster answered his call. His armies won battles, and the English seemed to be on the run.

In the end, though, the English were too strong. O'Neill got some help from abroad – a Spanish army landed in Ireland in 1601, but it was soon rounded up by the English. In 1603, O'Neill gave up the fight. Four years later, he left Ireland for good. By then, there were English governors and forts in all parts of Ireland – the conquest seemed complete.

Now try Exercises 6.3, 6.4, and 6.5.

A Dutch sixteenth-century drawing, showing an Irish peasant and a lady from the Pale

Exercise 6.3

Read **Sections B** and **C**.
What were the **causes** of the Irish revolts against the English? Copy the sentences and write TRUE or FALSE after each one.

a The Irish thought that the English were foreigners.

_____

b Irish law and English law were the same. _____

c The English did not understand the Irish language.

_____

d The Irish peasants soon became Protestants. _____

e 'Plantations' means growing trees in Ireland. _____

f Irish lords and peasants were angry about losing their land. _____

g Hugh O'Neill asked all Catholic Irishmen to join his revolt. _____

h The three main causes of the revolts were that the Irish did not want to be ruled by Englishmen, they wanted to remain Catholic, and they did not want to lose their land.

_____

Source 6e

The conquest was a good thing for Ireland. It gave her law and order. It ended the wars between the Irish tribes, the raids, and the killing. England's victory let the Irish grow into a nation.

Adapted from a book written by G. R. Elton in 1955.

Source 6f

At the end of the revolt, Ireland was in a dreadful state. The English had won, but the Irish were reduced to hunger and misery. Wolves roamed the countryside. Children crawled on all fours, eating grass. Some men and women were so hungry that they became cannibals.

Adapted from a book written by Sir Keith Feiling in 1927.

Source 6g

The Irish live like beasts in the mountains. Their homes are huts made of straw. The men are tall and broad, and can run like deer. They eat only once a day, at night. What they eat is usually butter with oatmeal bread. They drink sour milk, not water. There is no justice or law and order in the land – everyone does as he likes.

Written by a Spanish noble who was shipwrecked on the Irish coast in 1588.

Exercise 6.4

Read **Sources 6e** and **6f**.
Discuss these questions in a group, then write four paragraphs – one answering each of the questions.

a Which source says that conquest by the English was a good thing for Ireland? In what ways was it good?

b Which source says that conquest by the English was a bad thing for Ireland? In what ways was it bad?

c Which author was thinking of the short-term results of the conquest (i.e. what Ireland was like just after the English conquest)? Which author was thinking of the long-term results of the conquest (i.e. what happened in Ireland in the next hundred or two hundred years)?

d Is it possible that both authors were right?

Source 6h

The Irish peasants live in fear of attacks by robbers and rebels. So they make no attempt to grow crops. They roam about with their cows like nomads. They have no fixed homes, but sleep in the open, or in clay huts, or wooden cabins covered with turf. They light a fire in the middle of the hut, and sleep on the ground, with no bedding under them.

Written by Fynes Moryson, who was in Ireland in 1600.

Exercise 6.5

Read **Sources 6g** and **6h**.
Which of these things do **Sources 6g** and **6h** tell us about?

a The homes the Irish lived in.
b The language the Irish spoke.
c The clothes the Irish wore.
d The food the Irish ate.
e Irish schools.
f Law and order in Ireland.

Choose three topics from the list, and write brief notes (which you could later use as an essay plan) about each of them.

Henry VII, the first of England's Tudor Kings, had a Welsh grandfather. Henry was born at Pembroke Castle.

A The Acts of Union

The Norman **marcher lords** conquered east and south Wales after 1066. **King Edward I** conquered the rest of Wales between 1272 and 1300. But English rule did not bring peace and justice to Wales. Great lords, with their bands of armed men, bullied the peasants and stole their cattle. The courts were no help, for the lords and their men controlled them too.

In 1493, **King Henry VII** set up a **Council for Wales** to try to bring law and order where there was none. The Council did some good work, but only made a start. Then, in 1534, **Henry VIII** chose **Rowland Lee** to be the Council's head. He gave Lee the job of stamping out crime. And for the next nine years, Lee toured eastern Wales, torturing, hanging, and flogging. His victims were more often rich than poor, but he was hated by all.

Henry VIII's main plan for Wales, though, was **Union with England**. Two acts, passed by Parliament in 1536 and 1543, said that Wales and England were one. English law, they said, applied to Wales, so Welshmen had the same rights as Englishmen (which they had not had before). And Welsh members would sit in Parliament in London.

The Union was good for the poor of Wales. The courts became fair, the armed bands were crushed, and peace was restored. The Welsh gentry took the chance to move up in the world. The acts said that Welshmen could be magistrates (J.P.s), so long as they spoke English. So the gentry sent their sons to English schools, and became English in their ways.

Now try Exercises 7.1 and 7.2.

Exercise 7.1

Read **Section A** and the sentences below.
Ask the questions 'Who did it?' and 'When was it done?' about each of the sentences. Write your answers in a chart or table.

a They conquered south Wales.
b He conquered the rest of Wales.
c He set up a Council of Wales.
d He stamped out crime in eastern Wales.
e He got Parliament to pass the Acts of Union.
f They took the chance to become J.P.s.

A miniature portrait of Henry VIII from one of the first legal documents produced in the Welsh county of Brecon after the first Act of Union

Aims

Students of history try to find out the **aims** of the people in the past. This means asking, 'What were they **trying** to do?' or 'What were their **reasons** for acting as they did?'

For example, 'What were Henry VIII's aims when he got Parliament to pass the Acts of Union with Wales?'

Sometimes the people in the past have told us what their aims were. More often, we have to guess at their aims by looking at what they did. Not all authors agree about people's aims – see **Sources 7a** and **7b**.

Source 7a

The Acts of Union put Wales completely under English rule. Their aim was to crush the Welsh language and nation. Only those who knew English could take part in the government of Wales. (And only one Welshman in twenty could speak English.) The Welsh could enjoy the same rights as the English, but only if they stopped being Welsh.

Adapted from a book written by Gwynfor Evans in 1974.

Source 7b

Welshmen at the time did not object to the Acts of Union. For them, the really important thing was that Englishmen and Welshmen were now equal in law. Also, Welshmen no longer needed special permits to live in towns. The Acts did not try to crush the Welsh language. Their aim was to unite England and Wales. No-one was punished for speaking Welsh. Judges did not object when Welsh was used in their courts.

Adapted from a book written by W. Vaughan-Thomas in 1985.

Exercise 7.2

Read **Sources 7a** and **7b**, and the note on 'Aims'. Then answer the questions in sentences.

a Write down any facts that you can find in **Source 7a**.

b What was the aim of the Acts of Union, according to **Source 7a**?

c What does the author of **Source 7a** think about the Acts of Union?

d Write down any facts that you can find in **Source 7b**.

e What was the aim of the Acts of Union, according to **Source 7b**?

f What does the author of **Source 7b** think about the the Acts of Union?

Source **7c**

Tintern Abbey in Monmouth

B From Reformation to Methodism

The Welsh did not complain when Henry VIII took the Pope's place as head of the Church in 1534. They did not object when he closed the monasteries. But they were not pleased when pilgrimages to saint's shrines were banned. For the Welsh were proud of their ancient saints.

The main event of the Reformation in Wales, though, was the translation of the Bible into Welsh. (Look at **Source 7e**.) Most of the people of Wales spoke only Welsh, and understood neither Latin nor English. Now they could understand when the Bible was read to them in church. (Very few could read it for themselves.) The translation gave a boost to the Church, and a boost to Welsh.

Source **7d**

Ewenny Priory in Glamorgan

Henry VIII closed down the monasteries in Wales, as well as in England. Tintern Abbey (**Source 7c**) fell into ruins. Ewenny Priory (**Source 7d**) became a country house.

Source **7e**

The title page of the first Bible in Welsh, published in 1588

By the time of Queen Anne (1702–1714), though, the Church in Wales had become poor and backward. All the bishops were English, and some of them did not even visit Wales. The priests were badly paid, and ignorant – many of them knew no Welsh. Even the buildings were falling down.

Methodist preachers like **Howell Harris** tried to put life back into the Church. In the 1730s and 1740s, they travelled through Wales, preaching outdoors, in Welsh, often two or three times a day. Excited crowds listened, and sang, shouted, and clapped. The English called them 'Welsh Jumpers', and said that they were mad. But the movement grew into a Church that gripped the whole of Wales.

Now try Exercise 7.3.

'Welsh Jumpers' – early Methodists

Exercise 7.3

Read **Section B** and look at **Sources 7c**, **7d**, and **7e**. Write notes (in your own words), describing:

a **Three** important things that happened to the Church in Wales in the **sixteenth century**.
b The state of the Church in Wales in the **eighteenth century**, and how some people tried to improve it.

C Farmers and miners

Until long after 1750, Wales was a country of farmers. Some of them grew crops, such as wheat and barley, for bread and beer. Most of them grew leeks, cabbages, peas and beans for themselves and their families. But to all Welsh farmers, their animals mattered most.

Peace and order followed the Acts of Union. This was good for Welsh farmers, for the cattle-thieves had been stamped out. **Drovers** could now walk herds of cattle slowly along the tracks and roads from north Wales to London. As London grew, so the demand for Welsh beef grew too. By 1750 as many as 30,000 cattle a year went over the border to England.

Welsh drovers with a herd of cattle on the way to England

On the hills, the Welsh kept sheep, chiefly for the wool. In the Middle Ages, the farmers sold the wool in English markets. After about 1500, though, the Welsh did more spinning, weaving and knitting themselves. In 1750, Welsh knitted woollen stockings were fashionable in England.

Some peasants mined coal as well as working on the land. (Men had dug for coal in south Wales since the Middle Ages.) As demand grew, more and more Welsh coal was sent by ship to Bristol or France or Ireland. Iron ore was also mined in south Wales. And after 1600, foundries in Cardiff were making cast-iron guns.

Apart from some fighting in the Civil War (see Chapter 8), Wales enjoyed peace between 1500 and 1750. Peace was good for everyone, and the population grew steadily, from 225,000 in 1550 to 480,000 in 1750. In that time, the gentry grew richer, and more English. The peasants remained poor, and stayed Welsh.

Now try Exercises 7.4 and 7.5.

Source 7f

Our subjects in south Wales are so poor that they do not send their sons to school. In any case, there are no schools in those parts. The result is that Welshmen of all ages and every class do not know God's laws. They do not know the law of the land either. And they do not know any English, so they do not understand the laws which they are supposed to obey.

Henry VIII's order to open a school at Brecon in 1541.

Exercise 7.4

Read **Section C**, and ask yourself the question, 'Which things changed, and which things stayed the same?' Copy the sentences and write **TRUE** or **FALSE** after each one.

a Most Welsh people made their living from farming between 1500 and 1750. _____

b The Acts of Union made things worse for the farmers. _____

c The number of Welsh cattle sold in England increased between 1500 and 1750. _____

d The Welsh farmers stopped keeping sheep after 1500. _____

e Coal-mining in Wales did not begin until after 1600. _____

f Iron guns were made in Cardiff in the seventeenth and eighteenth centuries. _____

g The population of Wales more than doubled between 1500 and 1750. _____

h The peasants continued to speak Welsh between 1500 and 1750. _____

Exercise 7.5

Read **Source 7f**. What were Henry VIII's **aims** when he set up the school at Brecon? Look at the list below, then write out the aims which you think are the same as Henry VIII's.

a To teach the children the Welsh language.
b To set up schools where there were none.
c To provide free schooling for the sons of Welshmen.
d To teach Welsh people God's commandments.
e To teach Welsh boys to speak English.
f To teach Welsh boys to read and write in English.
g To teach mathematics and science.
h To make sure that the people of Wales understood and obeyed the laws.

8 The Civil War

A Puritans and the Church of England

The **Puritans** (see page 20) were unhappy with the Church of England. They thought that there was no need for bishops as well as priests. They did not want priests to wear special robes. They did not like having to use a Prayer Book. In all these ways, they said, the Church of England was too close to the Catholic Church.

In 1603, King James VI of Scotland became **James I** of England. (Look at the family tree on page 24.) The English Puritans were pleased, for James had been brought up in Scotland by strict Protestants, men like themselves. So the Puritans hoped that he would alter the Church of England to suit them. But they were disappointed. James I made no changes.

In 1625, James died and **Charles I**

became king. The Puritans did not trust him, for his queen was a Catholic, and they thought he had plans to make the Church of England Catholic too. Priests made the sign of the cross as they prayed, and used altars instead of simple tables. William Laud, whom Charles chose to be Archbishop of Canterbury, sent inspectors round the churches to make sure that the Prayer Book was used. Puritans who broke the rules were put in prison.

When Charles tried to make the Scots use the Prayer Book in 1637, they rebelled. (See Chapter 12.) A Scots army invaded England, and took Newcastle. Charles had to pay them £850 a day to advance no further.

Now try Exercise 8.1.

Source  **8a**

Of God,   Of Man,   Of the Divell.

A cartoon from the time of James I. It shows a Puritan minister holding a Bible (left), a Church of England bishop holding a Prayer Book (centre) and a Catholic bishop holding a Mass Book (right).

Thomas Percy Guido Fawkes Robert Catesby

In 1605 there was a Catholic plot to blow up Parliament while King James I was present. The plot was discovered and the plotters were executed. The most famous plotter was Guy Fawkes.

Exercise 8.1

Read **Section A**, and study **Source 8a**.
Copy the sentences filling in the blank spaces as you go.

a The artist says that the Puritan minister stands for _____'s religion.

b He says that the Church of England bishop stands for _____'s religion.

c He says that the _____ bishop stands for the devil's religion.

d The Puritan minister is holding a _____

e The Church of England bishop is holding a _____ Book, and the Catholic bishop is holding a _____ Book.

f Apart from the books they are holding, there is no difference between the _____ of _____ and the _____ bishops.

g The artist is saying that there is not much difference between the _____ Church and the Church of _____

h The artist must have been a _____

King Charles I

B Parliament and Taxes

James I and Charles I were always short of money. Most of what they spent came from the people, as taxes passed by **Parliament**. The gentry and merchants who sat in the House of Commons did not much like their Stuart kings. They said that they both wasted money, and would not agree to all they wanted.

The quarrel between Charles I and the Commons was so bad that after 1629 the king tried to rule without Parliament. He collected some taxes without Parliament's permission. Men who refused to pay were fined or put in prison.

Some gentry thought that Charles

was becoming a **despot** – a ruler who ignored the law. His governor of Ireland, the tough **Earl of Strafford**, did ignore the law. (See Chapter 13.) In 1639, Charles ordered Strafford to return to England and take command. The gentry grew even more alarmed.

King Charles, on the other hand, thought that ruling the country was **his** job, not the people's. Most other countries had kings who were above parliaments and the law. Why should England be different?

Parliament met in 1640 because King Charles needed money to pay the Scots. (See Section A.) The House of Commons was full of men who objected to what Charles had done. They said that in future the king must not rule without Parliament. They condemned Strafford to death. Then they began to attack the Church of England as well. Charles could stand no more. In 1642 civil war broke out between him and Parliament.

Now try Exercises 8.2 and 8.3.

Exercise 8.2

Read **Section B**.
On the left side of the page below, you will see the **first halves** of seven sentences on the causes of the Civil War. On the right side are the **second halves**, but in a different order. Put the correct halves together, and write out the complete sentences.

First halves

a The members of the House of Commons thought that . . .
b After 1629, Charles I made people . . .
c Some gentry accused Charles I . . .
d A lot of people said that the Earl of Strafford had . . .
e Charles I thought that it was the king's duty . . .
f Charles I had to call Parliament in 1640 . . .
g Civil war broke out in 1642 because Charles I . . .

Second halves

● objected to the changes Parliament was making.
● of trying to make himself a despot.
● because he needed money for the war with Scotland.
● to rule the country as he thought fit.
● James I and Charles I did not spend their money wisely.
● behaved like a despot in Ireland.
● pay taxes without asking for Parliament's consent.

Source 8b

Strafford was a would-be tyrant. He said that Parliament had gone too far, and he wanted to set King Charles free from its controls. He thought that the king had a right to absolute power. And he saw that the only way of giving him that power was by force, and fear.

Adapted from a book written by John Richard Green in 1874.

The House of Commons in the seventeenth century

Source 8c

Strafford said that the king was the 'father' of the country. It was his job to look after the people in it. To do his job properly, he had to be strong. He must not let the gentry and lawyers in Parliament take his powers away. His servants must work hard to keep justice and order. 'Less than Thorough (see page 65) will not do', as he said.

Adapted from a book written by Sir Keith Feiling in 1927.

Exercise 8.3

Read **Sources 8b** and **8c**.
Discuss these questions in a group:

a Who wrote the two sources, and when were they written? Are they primary or secondary sources?
b Both sources tell us how Strafford wanted England to be governed. What sort of government did he want? Do the two sources give us the same answer to this question?
c What did Strafford think about the Members of Parliament? Do the two sources give us the same answer to this question?
d Is **Source 8b** on Strafford's side, against him, or neutral? (Give some reasons for your opinions.)
e Is **Source 8c** on Strafford's side, against him, or neutral? (Give some reasons for your opinions.)

After discussing the questions, either **i** Write your answers in a short essay in your own words, or **ii** Make a group tape.

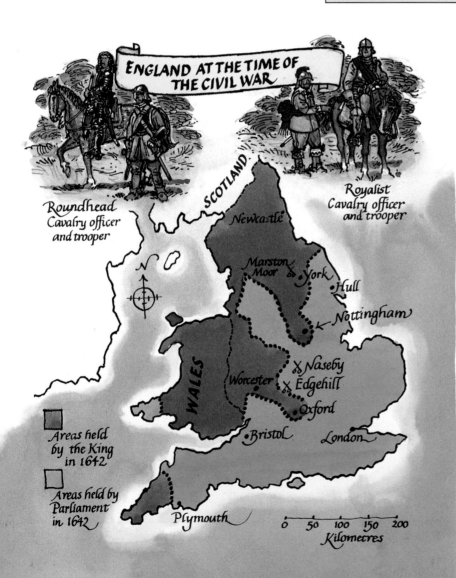

ENGLAND AT THE TIME OF THE CIVIL WAR

Roundhead Cavalry officer and trooper

Royalist Cavalry officer and trooper

SCOTLAND

Newcastle

Marston Moor · York · Hull

· Nottingham

WALES

Worcester · Naseby · Edgehill · Oxford

· Bristol · London

Plymouth

Areas held by the King in 1642

Areas held by Parliament in 1642

0 50 100 150 200
Kilometres

C Cavaliers and Roundheads

Charles left London and in August 1642, he raised his standard above Nottingham Castle. This was a signal that all men who were loyal to the king should prepare to fight for him. The Civil War was about to begin. (The king's army were called the **Cavaliers**.)

Parliament's leaders did not want to get rid of the king, but they could not trust Charles I. He had to be made less powerful. So they too raised an army. It was called the **Roundhead** army, because many of the men were Puritans, and Puritans cut their hair short.

The two armies were about equal at first. The Cavaliers had better cavalry, commanded by the king's nephew from Germany, Prince Rupert. They tried to advance on London, but failed. Then the Roundheads, with help from the Scots, started to win.

In 1644 and 1645 the Roundheads formed the **New Model Army**, a force of well drilled and well armed troops.

They were properly paid, and their officers were men who knew their job. The New Model Army won the Battle of Naseby for Parliament in June 1645, and the war ended in 1646. Charles gave himself up to the Scots, and they handed him over to Parliament.

Charles I could have remained king if he had agreed to share his power with Parliament. But he tried to be clever. He escaped and made a deal with the Scots, who promised to put him back in control. A Scots army invaded England in 1648, but it was beaten by **Oliver Cromwell** and the New Model Army. Cromwell and the other generals were now in charge.

Now try Exercises 8.4 and 8.5.

A pikeman

Exercise 8.4

Read **Section C**.
Write sentences to show that you know what these words mean:

Standard   Civil War   Cavaliers   Roundheads   Cavalry
Infantry   Officers   Generals

Source 8d

My own regiment of foot (infantry), at push of pike, forced back the enemy's strongest regiment. In the meantime, the cavalry beat back all the other side. They charged through the enemy's cavalry and their foot.

From Oliver Cromwell's account of a battle fought in 1650.

Exercise 8.5

Study the pictures on page 42 and **Source 8e**, and read **Source 8d**.

a Write notes about the following:
  i How Civil War soldiers were dressed.
  ii How pikemen marched, and how they fought in battle.
  iii How the cavalry fought in battle.
b Draw pictures (pin-men if you wish) showing pikemen
  i marching, and **ii** in battle.

Source 8e

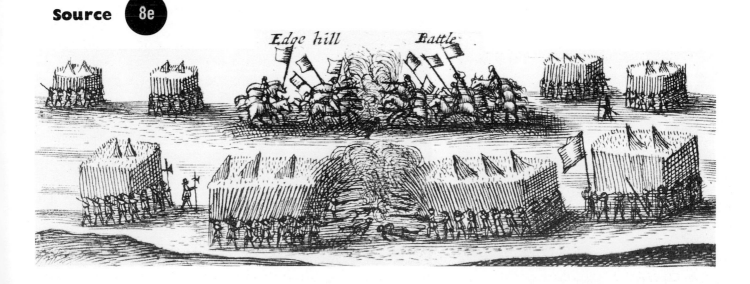

Edge hill Battle

9 The Commonwealth

A The English Republic

At the end of the Civil War, power was in the hands of the House of Commons. (Most of the House of Lords had sided with the king.) The Commons decided to make England a **Commonwealth**, or republic. It announced that in future there would be no king, and no House of Lords.

It was the Commons that put King Charles on trial. They charged him with making war on his people. Charles refused to answer the charge. He said that he was king, and only God could judge him. The court did not agree. It found him guilty and sentenced him to death. He was beheaded in front of a big crowd outside Whitehall Palace on 30th January 1649.

The army took its orders from the House of Commons. But the army's generals had got used to **giving** orders, not **taking** them. Before long, it was clear that the **army** was really in charge. The most powerful man in England was the leading general, **Oliver Cromwell**.

In 1653, Cromwell quarrelled with the members of the Commons, and threw them out. Later that year, he agreed to become **Lord Protector**, or

Oliver Cromwell

The execution of Charles I in 1649

head of the State. Some men even wanted to make him 'King Oliver'. He might have agreed, but the other generals would not stand for it.

At one stage, Cromwell split England and Wales into eleven districts, and put a major-general in charge of each of them. They kept good order, but the people did not like being ruled by soldiers. Not even Charles I had done that.

Now try Exercise 9.1.

Exercise 9.1

Read **Section A**, then answer the questions.

a Who was in charge of England at the end of the Civil War?
b What did 'Commonwealth' mean?
c When Charles I was put on trial, he was accused of doing what?
d Charles I said that the court had no right to try him. Why?
e What happened to the House of Commons in 1653?
f In which year did Cromwell take the title 'Lord Protector'?
g Why did Oliver Cromwell not become king?
h Why was government by the major-generals unpopular?

B The Commonwealth and its enemies

The family of Charles I fled abroad after the Civil War. But his eldest son, Prince Charles, hoped that he would return to England one day. Cromwell's army and navy kept watch to see that he did not.

Cromwell's first task was to deal with rebels in Ireland who took the side of Prince Charles. Cromwell and the army crossed to Ireland and crushed the revolt. The Irish people have hated the name Cromwell ever since. (See Chapter 13.)

The prince also got help from the Scots. They crowned him King Charles II in 1650. A Scots army invaded England, but Cromwell beat it at the Battle of Worcester. Roundhead troops searched for the prince after the battle, but he managed to escape to France. (See **Source 9a**.)

Cromwell had spies all over England, and secret agents abroad. Men who had fought for the king had to pay a special tax, and many lost their land. The major-generals had to watch **Royalists** (men known to be on the prince's side). Some of them banned horse-racing, so that there would be less chance for crowds to gather, and for the prince's friends to meet.

Now try Exercise 9.2.

Below: Commonwealth soldiers taking pictures out of a church, and breaking down altar rails

Below left: Prince Charles, later King Charles II

The Souldiers in their paſsage to York, turn unto reformers pull down Popiſh pictures, break down rayles, turn altars into Tables.

Source

Between the Battle of Worcester on 3rd September and going on board the ship at Brighton on 15th October, he travelled nearly 300 miles. He went sometimes on foot, and sometimes on a horse. Often he was disguised in coarse linen and a leather jacket. He had to spend one day in a barn, and another in a tree. He was glad to stay one night in a secret place at Boscobel which was never meant to be a king's bedroom. When he thought he was almost safe, he ran right into some of the rebels who were so greedy for his blood. Yet, thanks be to God, they did not recognize him.

From Thomas Blount's account of Prince Charles's escape.

Exercise 9.2

Read **Section B** and **Source 9a**. Write notes in answer to the questions.

a Which do you think are the five most important **facts** in **Source 9a**?

b Write down any **opinions** that you can find in Source 9a.

c Whose side was Thomas Blount on – the Commonwealth's or the prince's? Give reasons for your answer.

Source 9b

A Parliamentary cartoon showing a Royalist with a wolf's head and eagle's claws.

C Puritan England

Before the Civil War, the Puritans complained about the Church of England. Now the Puritans were on top. The Commons said that there would be no bishops, and the Prayer Book was banned. Statues and pictures were removed from churches. There were no more 'holy days'.

The law was strict about what was allowed on Sundays. No-one could travel on a Sunday, except to and from church. Shops and public houses were closed. Dancing and singing were banned. Sundays would have been very dull if all the rules had been kept, but they were not.

The major-generals had to make sure that there was no drunkenness or swearing, and that everyone went to church. They could close down theatres and public houses if they wished. Some of them used these powers, but others were not so hard.

Oliver Cromwell died in 1658. His son Richard took his place, but Richard was weak. He was not a soldier or a statesman. He soon gave up, and the army took control. It called a new Parliament, and the members invited Prince Charles to return to England to become King Charles II.

Now try Exercises 9.3, 9.4, 9.5, and 9.6.

Exercise 9.3

Read **Section C**, and look at **Sources 9b** and **9c**.
Now think about this question:

'Were the artists who drew these cartoons on the side of the Commonwealth or against it?'

Do not write out a full answer to the question. Just write an essay plan – notes for four or five paragraphs, saying what you can see in the cartoons, and what the cartoons tell you about the artists who drew them.

Source 9c

A Royalist cartoon, showing Oliver Cromwell and other leading men of the Commonwealth sitting in the 'Cabinet Council'. The Chairman of the Council is the devil!

Source 9d

People who go to the theatre know that we have put right a lot of things that were wrong. Bad language and rude jokes have been cut out of our plays now. We no longer make fun of famous men. Off the stage, actors have stopped borrowing money and cadging drinks from rich young men. These days, you never find an unruly mob or pick-pockets at a theatre.

A protest made in 1643 by some London actors who did not want Parliament to close the theatres.

Exercise 9.4.

Parliament closed the London theatres during the Civil War. Why did it do so? What were the **motives** of the Members of Parliament?
Read **Source 9d**, then copy the sentences below and fill in the blank spaces. The Members of Parliament objected to:

a Plays that contained _____ language and rude _____

b Plays that contained jokes about _____ _____

c Actors borrowing _____ from rich young men.

d Actors who _____ too much, and did not pay for their _____

e Disorderly crowds at _____

f _____ operating among the theatre crowds.

Source  **9e**

The soldiers and the Puritans thought he was wonderful. The Cavaliers hated him. I think he was modest most of the time, until success spoiled him. Then he gave in to temptation. He thought that God had made him great, and given him victory against the king. He thought that if God was with him, he must be always right. Pride made him selfish and greedy.

Written by Richard Baxter, a Puritan minister who knew Oliver Cromwell.

The sources do not all say the same

As you have seen, writers do not always say the same thing about the people of the past. There are many reasons why this may be so. Here are a few of them:

a Writers who met and talked to the people of the past knew more than writers who got what they knew from books.

b Authors of some **primary sources** had strong **opinions** – they took one side or the other.

c Authors of some **primary sources** took part in the events themselves. They tried to show that they had always been right.

d As time has passed, many sources have been lost or destroyed.

e Modern writers can read **all** the sources that remain. Some of these sources were kept secret in the past.

f Authors take the side of their own country. For example, English writers take the English point of view, and Irish writers take the Irish point of view.

Source **9f**

He was a modest man, keen to do his duty. His enemies said he was ambitious, of course. But he was not out for himself. He wanted, above all, to serve his country, understand his friends, and forgive his enemies. He did not often boast, though he got excited in battle. When victory was won, he gave thanks to the Lord and his men.

Adapted from a book written by Dr. Maurice Ashley in 1957.

Exercise 9.5

Read **Sources 9e** and **9f**, then read the sentences below. Write out the sentences which you think are true.

a Richard Baxter knew Cromwell, but Dr. Ashley is a twentieth-century writer.

b Both authors thought that Cromwell was a modest man.

c Richard Baxter thought that Cromwell was spoiled by his own success.

d Dr. Ashley thought that Cromwell was more concerned for his country than himself.

e Richard Baxter said that Cromwell thought God was always on his side.

f Both sources said that Cromwell believed that he was always right.

g Only Dr. Ashley said that Cromwell gave credit to God and his men.

g Both sources said that Cromwell became selfish and greedy.

i Richard Baxter said that success made Cromwell proud, and that pride made him selfish and greedy.

Exercise 9.6

Look again at **Sources 9e** and **9f**, read your answer to Exercise 9.5, and read the note 'The sources do not all say the same.'

Discuss this question in a group: 'Why do you think that Richard Baxter and Dr. Ashley had different opinions of Oliver Cromwell?'

After the discussion, either **a** Make a group tape (or a member of the group could give a talk); or **b** Write out your answer in a paragraph.

10 Restoration and Revolution

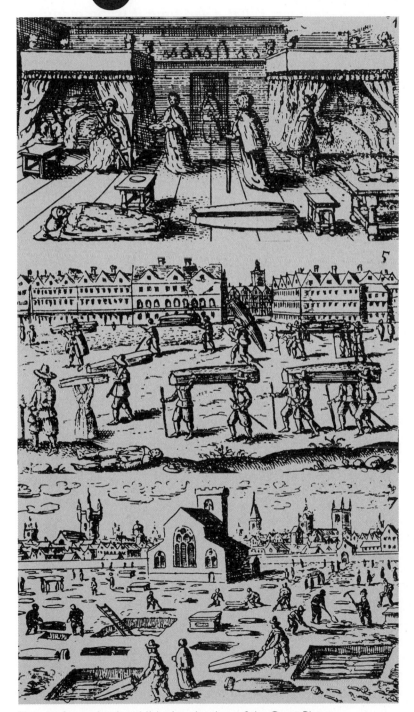

Pictures from a book published at the time of the Great Plague

A Plague and fire

Charles II was restored (allowed to return to England as king) in 1660. Most people were glad to have him back after the bleak years of the Commonwealth. The laws that made Sundays so dull were cancelled. In London, the theatres were open again.

For some people, London was a cheerful place in Charles II's reign. But it was also deadly dangerous. Disease was everywhere, and the smell must have been awful. The heaps of rubbish in the streets were perfect breeding-places for black rats. And the fleas that lived on the rats carried **bubonic plague**.

The plague had never gone away since the **Black Death** of 1348–9. Every few years there was an outbreak. In 1665, after a pause of 30 years, it swept London again, and nearly 70,000 people died. Those who could afford to do so fled, taking the disease with them.

Plague was highly infectious, and killed its victims within hours. Houses where it struck were locked and barred, and those inside could come out only at night. That was when the carts rumbled through the streets, and you could hear the mournful cry, 'Bring out your dead!'

By the end of 1665 the worst was over, and the plague did not come back. The reason was not that doctors found a cure. It was that **brown** rats drove out the black rats. Brown rats had different fleas, ones that did not carry plague.

A second disaster hit London in 1666. In five days in September, fire wiped out the city's heart. Wooden buildings burned easily, and there was no proper fire brigade. Men pulled down houses, or blew them up, to stop the fire spreading. For a second time, the rich and famous fled.

After the fire, a great chance was missed. London could have become a new, planned city with wide streets and proper sewers. But the houses were put up just as before, with no thought for health or hygiene. On the other hand, fine new churches were built, to **Sir Christopher Wren's** designs. His greatest work was the new **St. Paul's Cathedral**.

Now try Exercises 10.1 and 10.2.

Source

7th June. I saw two or three houses in Drury Lane marked with a red cross on the doors, and 'Lord have mercy upon us' written there. It was the first time I had seen that.

12th July. So many are dying that they have to bury some in daylight. (There is not time to bury them all at night.)

15th September. What a sad time it is! So many people have left London that there are no boats on the river, and grass is growing in Whitehall court.

26th October. The town is beginning to be lively again, though the streets are still empty, and most of the shops are shut.

From the diary of Samuel Pepys.

Source

Number of deaths from plague in London in 1665.

May	*43*	*September*	*26,219*
June	*590*	*October*	*14,373*
July	*4,127*	*November*	*3,451*
August	*19,046*	*December*	*940*

Exercise 10.1

Read **Section A** and **Sources 10b** and **10c**, and study **Source 10a**.

a Put the halves of the sentences together, then write out the complete sentences.

First half of sentence.

i Pepys (**Source 10b**) first saw signs of plague in June, but **Source 10c** shows...

ii **Sources 10b** and **10c** agree that the greatest number of deaths occurred...

iii **Sources 10a** and **10b** both tell us that...

iv Only **Source 10a** shows...

v **Source 10c** tells us that the number of deaths fell in October, and **Source 10b** says...

vi We can see what it was like inside a house hit by plague by...

b Draw a bar-graph of plague deaths in London, May to December 1665.

Second half of sentence.

● in the summer and autumn of 1665.
● some bodies were buried in daylight.
● looking at **Source 10a**.
● that there were some plague deaths in May.
● how and where the victims were buried.
● that London was getting back to normal then.

A fire engine from the time of the Fire of London

Exercise 10.2

Study the fire-engine.
Write notes, saying

a How you think the fire-engine worked;

b What you think was wrong with the fire-engine – why it would not work very well.

Sir Christopher Wren, who designed the new St. Paul's Cathedral (in the background) and many other churches

B Whigs and Tories

Charles II had spent twelve years abroad, while England was a republic. For the rest of his life, his main aim was to remain king of England. He said, 'I do not want to go on my travels again.'

To be secure, he had to stay on good terms with the most important of his subjects, the **nobles** and **gentry**. They forced Charles to share his power with **Parliament**. They had good reason, for the nobles controlled the House of Lords, and the gentry controlled the House of Commons.

Charles II was an **Anglican** – a member of the Church of England. (Secretly, he may have been a Catholic.) Most of the nobles and gentry were Anglicans. They disliked both Catholics and **Dissenters** – Protestants who did not belong to the Church of England. They got Parliament to pass acts which kept Catholics and Dissenters out of all the top jobs.

Charles II had no children. His heir was his brother **James**, who was a Catholic. None of the nobles and gentry liked the idea that the next king would be a Catholic. One group (called the **Whigs**) wanted to pass a bill saying that James could not be king. But the others (called the **Tories**) said that James was the heir, and had a right to be king.

Charles took his brother's side. With the help of the Tories, he made the Whigs give in. And when Charles died in 1685, his brother took the throne as James II.

Now try Exercise 10.3.

King James II

C The Revolution of 1688

The Whigs were always against James II, because he was a Catholic. The Tories, at first, were on his side. They began to change their minds when James said that he wanted a full-time army. Both Whigs and Tories were afraid that a king with a **standing army** would have too much power.

When James put Catholics in command of the army, the Whigs and Tories grew more alarmed. He chose Catholics as his ministers, too. The Whigs and Tories, who were all Anglicans, were angry at being pushed out of these top jobs.

Parliament had passed laws against Catholics and Dissenters in high office. But James said that the laws did not apply. The Whig and Tory lords were furious – **Parliament** made the law, and **they** controlled Parliament. The king was taking their powers away.

James II, whose first wife was dead, had no sons. His two daughters were both Protestants. In time, he would die, and England would have a Protestant queen again. But James took a second wife, a Catholic. In June 1688 she gave birth to a **prince**. The prince would be a Catholic, and he was James's heir. (Look at the cartoon.)

The Whigs turned to **William of Orange** for help. William was the husband of James's elder daughter, and a Protestant. In November 1688, William and his army sailed from Holland to Devon. As he marched on London the nobles and gentry, Whig and Tory, took his side. James, finding himself with no friends, fled. Parliament said that he had resigned the crown, and offered it jointly to William and his wife Mary.

Now try Exercises 10.4 and 10.5.

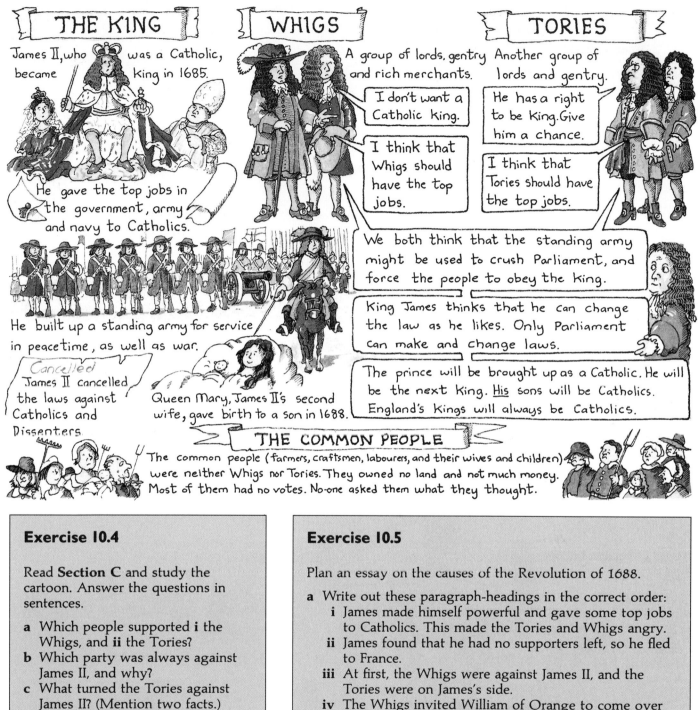

THE KING

James II, who was a Catholic, became king in 1685.

He gave the top jobs in the government, army and navy to Catholics.

He built up a standing army for service in peacetime, as well as war.

Cancelled
James II cancelled the laws against Catholics and Dissenters.

WHIGS

A group of lords, gentry and rich merchants.

I don't want a Catholic king.

I think that Whigs should have the top jobs.

TORIES

Another group of lords and gentry.

He has a right to be King. Give him a chance.

I think that Tories should have the top jobs.

We both think that the standing army might be used to crush Parliament, and force the people to obey the king.

King James thinks that he can change the law as he likes. Only Parliament can make and change laws.

The prince will be brought up as a Catholic. He will be the next King. His sons will be Catholics. England's Kings will always be Catholics.

Queen Mary, James II's second wife, gave birth to a son in 1688.

THE COMMON PEOPLE

The common people (farmers, craftsmen, labourers, and their wives and children) were neither Whigs nor Tories. They owned no land and not much money. Most of them had no votes. No-one asked them what they thought.

Exercise 10.4

Read **Section C** and study the cartoon. Answer the questions in sentences.

a Which people supported **i** the Whigs, and **ii** the Tories?
b Which party was always against James II, and why?
c What turned the Tories against James II? (Mention two facts.)
d Why did the Whigs and Tories think that the birth of a prince in 1688 was so important?
e How was William of Orange related to James II?
f Who asked William of Orange to help them?
g Why did James II leave England?
h What part did the common people play in the Revolution of 1688?

Exercise 10.5

Plan an essay on the causes of the Revolution of 1688.

a Write out these paragraph-headings in the correct order:
  i James made himself powerful and gave some top jobs to Catholics. This made the Tories and Whigs angry.
  ii James found that he had no supporters left, so he fled to France.
  iii At first, the Whigs were against James II, and the Tories were on James's side.
  iv The Whigs invited William of Orange to come over from Holland.
  v The queen gave birth to a son in June 1688.
b Write out any one paragraph in full. (Use your own words.)

From Stuart to Hanover

A The end of the Stuarts

James II was **deposed** (thrown out) mainly because he was a Catholic. The Protestant William and Mary took his place, but James always hoped to return. At first, there seemed a good chance that he would succeed, for he got help from King Louis XIV of France. So Parliament agreed to taxes to pay for a war with France. And it passed a law which said that no Catholic could be king or queen of England.

William and Mary had no children. When William died in 1702, the last Protestant Stuart, Mary's sister **Anne**, became queen. Anne had eleven children, but they all died young. So there was no Protestant Stuart heir when Anne died in 1714.

In the time of Queen Anne, the Whigs and Tories were at odds again. Both sides wanted power for themselves, as the queen's ministers. They quarrelled about the war with France, which was still going on. And they fought about the **succession** – who

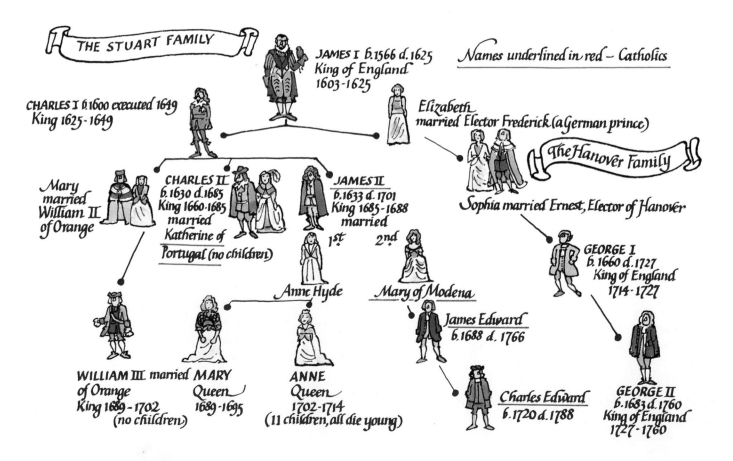

THE STUART FAMILY

JAMES I b.1566 d.1625
King of England
1603-1625

Names underlined in red – Catholics

CHARLES I b.1600 executed 1649
King 1625-1649

Elizabeth
married Elector Frederick (a German prince)

The Hanover Family

Mary
married
William II
of Orange

CHARLES II
b.1630 d.1685
King 1660-1685
married
Katherine of
Portugal (no children)

JAMES II
b.1633 d.1701
King 1685-1688
married

1st   2nd

Sophia married Ernest, Elector of Hanover

GEORGE I
b.1660 d.1727
King of England
1714-1727

Anne Hyde

Mary of Modena

James Edward
b.1688 d.1766

WILLIAM III married MARY
of Orange   Queen
King 1689-1702 1689-1695
(no children)

ANNE
Queen
1702-1714
(11 children, all die young)

Charles Edward
b.1720 d.1788

GEORGE II
b.1683 d.1760
King of England
1727-1760

54

should be king when Queen Anne died?

Some Tories would have liked **James Edward Stuart** (James II's son) on the throne. But the law said the king must be a Protestant, and James Edward was a Catholic. The Whigs wanted the Protestant **George**, elector (ruler) of **Hanover** in Germany, and got their way. When Anne died, 'German George' became king. (Look at the family tree.)

A few Tories would have liked the Stuarts to return. (People on the side of the Stuarts were called **Jacobites** at that time.) There were Jacobite risings in 1715 and 1745, and they had some success in Scotland. (See Chapter 12.) But in England, the Protestant Hanovers, with their Whig ministers, were firmly in control.

Now try Exercise 11.1.

William of Orange, later King William III of England and his wife, Mary (James II's daughter)

Exercise 11.1

Read **Section A**, and look at the family tree. Then write sentences to show that you know what these words and phrases mean:

a To depose the king. **b** Catholic.
c Protestant. **d** The Stuart family.
e The king's (or queen's) ministers. **f** The succession.
g The elector of Hanover. **h** The Jacobites.

B The victory of the Lords

In 1689, Parliament passed acts which took power from the king (or queen). They said that only Parliament could change the law – the king could not do it alone. Taxes were legal only if Parliament agreed to them. There could be a **standing army**, but it too needed parliament's consent. And that consent had to be given **each year**. This meant that Parliament had to meet at least once a year. Therefore, the king or queen could not rule without it.

Parliament said that it had a right to these powers because it spoke for the people. In fact, it spoke for a few of the people – the rich ones, those who owned the land. These were the nobles who sat in the House of Lords, and the gentry who sat in the Commons.

The House of Commons was **elected**. But not many men (and no women) had the right to vote. Men who could vote had to do so in public, so their landlords and employers could see how they voted, and **force** them to vote the right way. Those who could not be forced might be **bribed**.

The forcing and bribing were done by men with land and money – the gentry and the nobles. The most powerful men were the richest, and they were the nobles, with their huge estates. That is why the House of Lords was more important than the Commons at this time. Many of the gentry in the Commons followed the orders of nobles in the Lords.

Now try Exercise 11.2.

An election to choose the Member of Parliament for Oxford, held in Oxford Town Hall in 1687. Only a small number of people had the right to vote, and they did not vote in secret.

Exercise 11.2

Read **Section B**, then copy the sentences and write TRUE or FALSE after each one.

a Acts passed in 1689 made the king (or queen) stronger. _____

b The king had to call a meeting of Parliament each year, so that he could ask for permission to keep a standing army. _____

c Kings could no longer rule without Parliament. _____

d Most men, and some women, had the right to vote. _____

e People could not vote in secret.

_____

f Some employers sacked their workers if they voted for the wrong man. _____

g The House of Commons was more important than the House of Lords in the eighteenth century.

_____

h The gentry were the owners of the biggest estates. _____

C Cabinet and Prime Minister

King George I

In the time of William and Mary, the king was still the head of the Government. William had ministers to help him, of course. But he chose them, and he could sack them. The king made the big decisions, such as when to go to war.

Queen Anne, George I and George II still had a lot of power. They picked their own ministers, and discussed Government business with them. But they learned that they could not do just as they pleased.

After 1688, the ministers had to ask Parliament **each year** to agree to taxes and the army bill. And if Parliament did not like the king's ministers or what they did, it might not pass these bills. So the king or queen had to pay attention to Parliament, and to the great lords who controlled it. (See Section B.)

The king or queen and the chief ministers met once a week in the **Cabinet**. William attended the Cabinet when he was in England (he was often away at war). Queen Anne was always there. So was George I, for the first three years of his reign.

After 1717, the Cabinet usually met without the king. When it did so, one of the ministers was chairman. After the meeting, he went to the king and told him what the Cabinet advised. **Sir Robert Walpole** did this job from 1722 to 1742. He was the head of the king's government – Britain's first **Prime Minister**.

Now try Exercises 11.3, 11.4 and 11.5.

Exercise 11.3

Read **Section C**, and look at the cartoons.
Make your own notes answering the questions below.

a Compare the '1620' cartoon with the '1705' cartoon:
  i What had changed?
  ii What had not changed?
b Compare the '1705' cartoon with the '1750' cartoons:
  i What had changed?
  ii What had not changed?

1620 King James I asked his <u>Council</u> for advice.

The King made the decisions.

1705 Queen Anne attended meetings of her <u>Cabinet</u>.

The Queen and the Cabinet made decisions together. No Prime Minister.

1750 The Cabinet made the decisions. The Prime Minister was the chairman.

The Prime Minister told King George II what the Cabinet had decided.

The Duke of Marlborough (seated), who led the British armies to victory in the wars against the French in Queen Anne's reign, and his chief engineer

Source 11a

For a long time, the Duchess of Marlborough was Queen Anne's closest friend. But the duchess got ruder and ruder, and in the end the queen could stand her no more. The queen found a new friend, Mrs Masham, a cousin of the Tory leader Harley. The queen told the duchess to leave the court, and there was a great row. Before she left, the duchess wrecked her rooms in St. James's Palace. The Whig ministers were dismissed soon after. Harley and the Tories took their place.

Adapted from a book written by Sir Charles Oman in 1895.

Source  11b

Princess (later Queen) Anne with one of her children. The princess posed for this portrait in 1694. It was painted by Sir Godfrey Kneller.

Source 11c

Sarah, Duchess of Marlborough. This portrait was painted from life in about 1700. The name of the artist is not known.

Source  11d

The cunning Harley found a way to turn the queen against the Duke of Marlborough. He introduced the queen to Mrs Masham, who became her close friend, and a rival to the duchess. In 1710, Mrs. Masham got the queen to break with the duchess. Soon after, she dismissed the Whigs and brought in Harley and the Tories.

Adapted from a book written by G. M. Trevelyan in 1904.

The Duke of Marlborough was a supporter of the Whigs and an opponent of the Tories led by Harley. As a result of the argument between Queen Anne and the Duchess of Marlborough, the Whigs lost power at court.

Exercise 11.4

Look at **Sources 11b** and **11c**, and read **Sources 11a** and **11d**.

a Answer these questions in sentences or write 'not known':
   i Who painted **Source 11b**, and when?
   ii Did the artist who painted **Source 11b** see Princess (later Queen) Anne?
   iii Who painted **Source 11c**, and when?
   iv Did the artist who painted **Source 11c** see the Duchess of Marlborough?
   v Who wrote **Source 11a**, and when?
   vi Who wrote **Source 11d**, and when?
   vii Which **sources** (**11a**, **11b**, **11c**, **11d**) are primary, and which are secondary?
b Draw a cartoon to show any event described in **Source 11a** or **11d**.

Exercise 11.5

Read carefully through **Sources 11a** and **11d** again. Then write two paragraphs about these two sources, answering these questions:

a In which ways do the two accounts say the same things?
b In which ways are the two accounts different?

12 Scotland in the Seventeenth and Eighteenth Centuries

A The National Covenant

King James VI of Scotland moved south to England as soon as he heard that Queen Elizabeth was dead. From 1603 until his death in 1625 he was king of England **and** king of Scotland. But in those twenty-two years he came back north only once.

James preferred England. The English lords obeyed the king, and were not always at war with each other. England was a richer land, so the king was better off. (He soon had a crowd of courtiers, English and Scots, keen to flatter him in return for gifts and favours.) Also, James thought Scotland's **Presbyterian** church was dull and boring. He much preferred the Church of England, with its bishops, Prayer Book, and priests in robes.

James brought back bishops in Scotland. In 1637, his son, Charles I, went further, and ordered that the Scots had to use a Prayer Book. This caused a huge storm – nobles, gentry, and townspeople joined in the protest. In 1638, they drew up the **National Covenant**, which said that they would not stand for changes in Scotland's Church. Charles tried to use force, but his army was beaten. In 1640 the Scots invaded the north of England.

The crisis that began with the Scottish Prayer Book led to the first Civil War. (See Chapter 8.) The Scots took the side of Parliament, and helped defeat the king. But in 1648 King Charles got the Scots to change sides. By then, though, the New Model Army was too strong. The Scots were beaten in the second Civil War, and King Charles went to his death.

Now try Exercises 12.1 and 12.2.

The Arch-Prelate of St Andrewes in Scotland reading the new Service-booke in his pontificalibus assaulted by men & Women, with Crickets stooles Stickes and Stones.

In 1637, Charles I ordered that a Prayer Book had to be used in churches in Scotland. This order caused riots, and was the main reason why the National Covenant was drawn up in 1638.

Craigievar Castle in Scotland

Exercise 12.1

Read **Section A**, then answer the questions in sentences.

a When did James VI of Scotland become king of England?
b Why did James prefer England to Scotland?
c What did James like about the Church of England?
d What change did James make in the Church of Scotland?
e What change did Charles I try to make in the Church of Scotland?
f What did the National Covenant say?
g Why did the row over the Prayer Book lead to the English Civil War? (Look back at Chapter 8, then write two or three sentences.)
h Which side did the Scots take in **i** the first Civil War, and **ii** the second Civil War?

Source 12a

The lords think that they are above the law. They mistreat the common people, and force the men to join their private armies. Then if they fall out with their neighbours, they start a war. It's one family against another, with not a thought for the king or the law.

From a book which King James VI wrote in 1597.

Exercise 12.2

Read **Source 12a.**

a Write down three **facts** from **Source 12a**.
b What do you think were King James's **opinions** about the Scottish lords? (Write one or two sentences.)

B Union with England

The Scots were angry about the execution of Charles I. In 1650, they crowned his son (Prince Charles) king of Scotland. But Cromwell would not permit that. He invaded Scotland, and beat the Scots army at Dunbar. When the Scots invaded England in the next year, Cromwell beat them again at Worcester. Charles II fled, and Scotland was occupied by English troops.

When Charles II was restored in England in 1660, he was restored in Scotland as well. When James II was deposed in England in 1688, he was deposed in Scotland also. England and Scotland had the same king, but that was all. They were not yet one country. Scotland had its own Parliament, laws, and Church.

In the time of Queen Anne, England's trade with its colonies was making it rich. (See Chapter 14.) Scotsmen had tried to found their own colony, but it failed. So Scottish merchants wanted the right to trade with England's colonies. The English were willing to agree to free trade, but at a price.

The price was accepting the English law on the **succession** (who should be the next king). The English were afraid that when Queen Anne died, England and Scotland would have different kings again. In England, **George of Hanover** was Queen Anne's heir, but the Scots had not made up their minds.

The Scots were not against George, but thought they had a right to choose their own king.

In 1707, agreement was reached on an **Act of Union**. It said that England and Scotland were to be one country – **Great Britain**. There would be one king or queen. (George of Hanover would be Queen Anne's heir). And there would be one Parliament. Trade between Scotland and England was to be free, and Scottish merchants could trade with English colonies. But Scotland kept its own Church, and its own laws and courts.

Now try Exercises 12.3 and 12.4.

Exercise 12.3

Read **Section B**. You will see that the English and Scots had different opinions and points of view. Make notes on

a Scottish opinions and points of view on
   i trade, and **ii** the succession.
b English opinions and points of view on
   i trade, and **ii** the succession.
c What the Act of Union said about
   i trade, **ii** the succession, **iii** Parliament, and **iv** the Scottish Church and laws.

The development of the first Union flag in 1707 from the Scottish and English flags. The English flag is on the left and the Scottish flag is in the middle.

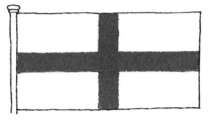  

Source 12b

> *For the English, the Union will make no change. They will keep the same Parliament, the same taxes, the same laws, and the same courts. But the Scots will have to pay the English debts, now and in the future. Scotland will lose the right to manage its own affairs. For the Scots, the Union will be a complete surrender.*

From a speech made by Lord Belhaven to the Scots Parliament in 1706.

Source   12c

> *For Scotland, the Union brought nothing but good. The farmers of the Lowlands learned new skills. Glasgow, which had been just a fishing port, grew into a rich and mighty city. Peace changed the wild men of the Highlands into peaceful herdsmen. The only thing the Scots lost was their old hatred of England.*

Adapted from a book written by the English historian J. R. Green in 1874.

Exercise 12.4

Read **Sources 12b** and **12c**, and discuss these questions in a group:

a What did Lord Belhaven think about the idea of an Act of Union? What results did he expect it to have, **i** for England, and **ii** for Scotland?
b What did J. R. Green (**Source 12c**) think about the results of the Act of Union? J. R. Green wrote his book how many years after the Act of Union was passed?
c Can you think of any **reasons** why there was such a difference between what Lord Belhaven expected and what later writers said about the Act of Union?

Then do one of the following:

i Make a group tape, giving your answers to the questions.
ii Make a wall-display, with pieces of written work and cartoons.

The
JACOBITE REBELLION
of 1745

Prince Charles Edward

The Duke of Cumberland
who defeated the Jacobites
at Culloden

→·→ Prince Charles carried
on French ship
- - → His advance from
Eriskay to Derby
←- - His retreat
⚔ Battle won by Jacobites
⚔ Battle lost by Jacobites

C **The Jacobites**

Many Scotsmen were against the Act of Union. Lowlanders said that Scotland would lose its freedom – Parliament in **London** would make laws and fix taxes for Scotland. A lot of Highlanders were against it as well. Their reason was that the Campbells, whom they hated, were for it.

In 1715, some of the clan chiefs rose in revolt against George I. Their aim was to make James VII's son **James Edward (the Pretender)** king instead. (They were called **Jacobites**.) Where the chiefs led, the clansmen followed, with sword in hand. But they did not get much support from the Lowlands or England, and the revolt fizzled out.

The second Jacobite revolt was more serious. Prince **Charles Edward**, the Pretender's son, raised his standard at Glenfinnan in August 1745. The chiefs obeyed the call, and a Highland army was formed. They took Edinburgh, beat King George's army at

Above: The Duke of Cumberland, the general who defeated the Jacobites at Culloden

Opposite page: The Battle of Culloden

Prestonpans, then marched into England. (Look at the map.)

There was panic in London. King George II prepared to leave for Germany. But not many Englishmen joined the prince. When he reached **Derby**, he could see that he had too few men to take London. In great sadness, he decided to turn back.

Charles retreated to Scotland with his tired and hungry Highlanders. The king's army advanced north to meet him. They met at **Culloden**, near Inverness. It was a slaughter, not a battle. The badly armed, exhausted Highlanders were cut down on the field, or in the flight that followed.

The prince escaped to the west, and by ship to France. His followers were hunted down. Some were hanged, others transported to the colonies for life. New laws said that Highlanders were not allowed to carry arms, wear the tartan, or play the bagpipes.

Now try Exercise 12.5.

Exercise 12.5

Read **Section C**, and look at the map.
Copy the passage below and fill in the blank spaces, using words from this list:

Dumfries York Glenfinnan Culloden Carlisle Orkney Eriskay Edinburgh French Glasgow Irish Derby Prestonpans Newcastle Skye Manchester

Prince Charles landed from a _____ ship on the island of _____ in the Outer Hebrides in August 1745. He crossed to the mainland, and raised his standard at _____, where a lot of Highlanders joined him. His army marched south, entered _____, and beat the king's army in battle at _____.

In November, they entered England and marched through _____ and _____. In December, they reached _____.

On their retreat, they went through Carlisle, _____, and _____ on the way to Inverness. At _____, in April 1746, the Jacobites were crushed by the king's army. Prince Charles fled to the west, and the island of _____. He set sail on a _____ ship in September 1746.

A Plantations and 'Thorough'

In the year that James I became king of England, revolt in Ireland ended. (See Chapter 6.) But James could not feel secure in Ireland. Most of the Irish were Catholics, and hated the Protestant English (and Scots). Revolt could break out again at any time. And England's enemies (such as Spain) might use Ireland as a base.

James I tried more **plantations**. He got about 20,000 Protestant settlers from England and Scotland to move to Ulster. Most of them were farmers, but some built new villages and towns, such as **Belfast**. And the London guilds that took over Derry changed its name to **Londonderry**.

A lot of Catholic Irish were driven out, and many lost their land. To them, the settlers were thieves. To the settlers, the Irish were wild beasts, or traitors, or both. The plantations were supposed to prevent revolt, but in fact they made it more likely.

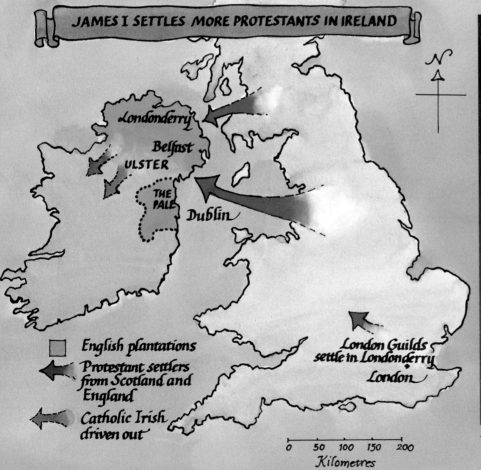

JAMES I SETTLES MORE PROTESTANTS IN IRELAND

Londonderry
Belfast
ULSTER
THE PALE
Dublin

☐ English plantations
← Protestant settlers from Scotland and England
← Catholic Irish driven out

London Guilds settle in Londonderry
London

0 50 100 150 200
Kilometres

The Earl of Strafford

Charles I's governor in Ireland was **Thomas Wentworth** (later **Earl of Strafford**). His aim was to keep Ireland quiet by making the king strong. This meant forcing the people to pay taxes and fines, and using the money to pay for an army.

Strafford called his policy 'Thorough' – he meant **tough**. He forced the Irish Parliament to pass extra taxes. He made landlords (Catholic and Protestant) pay fines, or face losing their land. He allowed Catholics to worship in their own way, in return for money. When Strafford returned to England, the Irish were glad to see him go. But the English thought that it was their turn next. (See Chapter 8.)

Now try Exercise 13.1.

Exercise 13.1

Read **Section A**, then look at the list of motives below. Decide **i** What were the motives of James I in Ireland?
ii What were the motives of Strafford in Ireland?

a He wanted to get more money out of the Irish.
b He wanted to make work for the unemployed from England.
c He did not want England's enemies to use Ireland as a base.
d He wanted to prevent another revolt in Ireland.
e He wanted to crush the Catholic Church.
f He wanted to be able to afford to keep an army in Ireland.
g He wanted the land to be properly farmed.
h He wanted to make the king strong.
i He wanted more Protestants in Ireland.

Write out James's motives and Strafford's motives in two columns.

B Rebellion and Civil War

The Ulster plantations did lead to more trouble. The Catholic landlords and peasants rose in revolt in 1641, and attacked the settlers who had taken their land. Protestants claimed that thousands of settlers were killed. But we now know that, at the same time, Protestant settlers were murdering Catholics.

The revolt spread to the whole of Ireland. In the 1640s, while King Charles I was at war with Parliament in England, there was civil war in Ireland too. But there it was Catholics against Protestants, and in most parts the Catholics came out on top.

As soon as Charles I was dead, the Commons turned to the problem of Ireland. They were worried that the Catholics there might do a deal with the late king's son. And with a base in Ireland, Prince Charles would be more of a threat to England.

They sent Oliver Cromwell and the army to Ireland. Cromwell crushed the rebels, but it was **how** he did so that made him hated. At **Drogheda**, 3,000 men, women, and children were killed by the soldiers. At **Wexford**, the same thing happened. Cromwell said that his actions saved lives – the other towns gave in without a fight. But the Irish never forgot.

Like James I, Cromwell tried to keep the peace in Ireland by means of **plantations**. But he went much further than King James. Cromwell said that Catholics could own land only in **Connaught** in the west. (Look at the map on page 29.) All the other land was given to former soldiers or sold to Protestants from England. The Catholics either moved to the west or became hired workers on what had been their own land.

Now try Exercise 13.2.

Source  **13a**

I think this is God's judgement on those barbarians who spilt so much innocent blood. Also, it will save lives in the future. These are good reasons for what was done. Otherwise, there would have been cause for sorrow and regret.

From a letter written by Oliver Cromwell after the massacre at Drogheda.

A cartoon of an English soldier raised for service in Ireland in the 1640s

Source **13b**

For the Irish, the way the revolt was crushed was the most important thing. Cromwell said that the massacre would save lives in the future. But in the long run it helped to make bitterness. And that caused far more blood to be spilt. Cromwell's name was branded on the memory of the Irish. To this day, it comes first to mind when Irishmen speak of the wrongs done to them.

Adapted from a book written in 1956 by Brian Inglis. The author grew up in Ireland, and used many Irish sources in his work.

Exercise 13.2

Read **Section B**, and **Sources 13a** and **13b**. Then answer the questions **a** to **f** in sentences, and question **g** in a paragraph.

a Who wrote **Source 13a**, and what was he doing in Ireland?

b Who did the author of **Source 13a** mean by 'barbarians who spilt so much innocent blood'? (Look at the first paragraph of **Section B**.)

c What did he mean by 'it will save lives in the future'? (Look at the fourth paragraph of **Section B**.)

d Who wrote **Source 13b**, and when? What was the author's connection with Ireland?

e On what important point do **Sources 13a** and **13b** disagree?

f What do you think the words 'Cromwell's name was branded on the memory of the Irish' (**Source 13b**) mean?

g Why do you think that **Sources 13a** and **13b** say different things about Cromwell in Ireland? (Look back to the note 'The sources do not all say the same' in Chapter 9.)

C Wild geese and penal laws

A few Irish Catholics got their land back when Charles II was restored in 1660. But the main hope of the Irish was the Catholic **James II**, who became king in 1685. Catholics got jobs as mayors, judges, and officers in the army. James' governor of Ireland was a Catholic. There was even talk of giving Catholics back their land.

Then came the revolution of 1688. (See Chapter 10.) James II fled from England, but he tried to make a comeback through Ireland. He got help from the French, landed at Kinsale in 1689, and soon nearly all of Ireland was in his hands.

Protestant **Londonderry** held out

against him, though. Then, in 1690, **William of Orange** himself came to Ireland, and beat James in the **Battle of the Boyne**. James fled again, and the '**wild geese**' followed. These were Catholics who had fought for James, and now left Ireland for good. Many of them later served in the armies of the king of France.

After 1690 came the Protestant '**Ascendancy**'. This was the time when the Protestants were in control, and showed that they meant to stay there. They passed a string of acts (called the '**penal laws**') which kept Catholics out of all the top jobs. They said that Catholics could not buy land, or keep weapons, or vote in elections. Catholic priests were allowed, but not bishops, and there were to be no Catholic schools.

Now try Exercises 13.3, 13.4, and 13.5.

James II appointed the Catholic Earl of Tyrconnell as his governor of Ireland. The Protestant playing-card calls him a 'knave'.

A modern Protestant wall painting of William of Orange

Exercise 13.3

Read **Section C**.

a Make rough notes of your own, listing all the Catholics' grievances (things they would have grumbled about) in Ireland in 1750.
b Discuss your list with other pupils in a group. See if you have missed any grievances that they have noticed.
c Make a group wall-display, with pieces of written work, drawings, and cartoons.

Exercise 13.4

Look at the charts which show who owned the land in Ireland between 1625 and 1750.

a Draw a graph, showing how much of the land in Ireland was owned by Catholics between 1625 and 1750.
b Write at least one sentence saying what the charts and your graph tell you.
c Try to find at least three facts in Chapter 13 explaining why the amount of land owned by Catholics changed. (Write three sentences.)

Who owned the land in Ireland, 1625–1750?

☐ Protestant
☐ Catholic

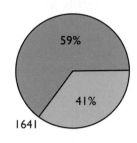

79%

21%

1625

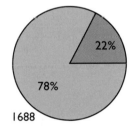

59%

41%

1641

22%

78%

1688

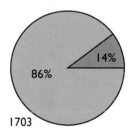

14%

86%

1703

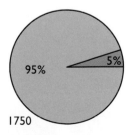

5%

95%

1750

In 1600, more than 90% of the population of Ireland was Catholic

In 1750, about 75% of the population of Ireland was Catholic

Source  13c

A stranger would not think that Ireland had fertile soil and a mild climate. He would see families living in filth on butter-milk and potatoes. He would see people without shoes or stockings on their feet, living in houses that are worse than English pig-styes. But this would not trouble him. He only comes for a short time, then goes back to England. And it is to England that all of Ireland's wealth is sent.

(This was written in 1727 by Jonathan Swift, who lived for many years in Ireland.)

Source  13d

An Irish peasant's cabin in the eighteenth century

Source 13e

Bantry House, County Cork – an eighteenth-century country house in Ireland

Exercise 13.5

Read **Source 13c**, and study **Sources 13d**, and **13e**. Copy the sentences below and write TRUE or FALSE after each of them.

a The author of **Source 13c** lived in Ireland. _____

b The author of **Source 13c** knew how Irish peasants lived. _____

c Everyone in Ireland probably lived in the way described in **Source 13c**. _____

d **Source 13c** does not say why Irish peasants were poor. _____

e **Source 13d** is a photograph of Irish peasants. _____

f **Sources 13c** and **13d** tell us the same kind of thing about Irish peasants. _____

g We should believe what **Sources 13c** and **13d** tell us. _____

h **Source 13e** shows a rich man's house, built in Ireland in the eighteenth century. _____

i **Source 13e** proves that some people in Ireland had a lot of money. _____

j **Source 13e** proves that **Sources 13c** and **13d** are wrong. _____

14 Trade and Colonies

Merchant ships trading in the East in the seventeenth century

A The East India Company

In 1500, **England** was a small country that did not count for much. By 1750, **Britain** (made up of England, Scotland, Wales, and Ireland) was a **great power** – one of Europe's leading states. This change took place because Britain grew rich from **trade**.

In the time of the Tudors, England's main trade was selling woollen cloth to Antwerp in the Low Countries (now Belgium). But the Low Countries belonged to the king of Spain. And when Queen Elizabeth I fell out with King Philip of Spain, he banned the English from Antwerp.

The merchants searched for new markets. Some sailed to Russia, and others to Turkey. In 1600, trade began with India. A group of London mer-

chants started the **East India Company**. Their money paid for the ships and the crews. It was their gold and silver which the ships carried on the outward journey. They paid for the trading stations which Indian rulers allowed them to set up in certain ports. (Look at the Map on pages 70–71.)

The risks were great – many a ship was lost in a storm or taken by pirates. Sometimes there was a fight at sea with the French or Dutch. But when a ship did come home, laden with Indian silks and cottons (and later China tea), the merchants got the profits. A successful voyage would pay their costs five times over.

Now try Exercise 14.1.

EUROPEAN COLONIES
IN THE AMERICAS
- English
- French
- Spanish
- Dutch
- Portuguese

Virginia

West Indies

SOU
AME

Exercise 14.1

Read **Section A** and study the Map.
Then copy the questions and write your answers in the spaces.

a What did English merchants sell in Antwerp?

_____

b Who banned English merchants from Antwerp?

_____

c When was the East India Company set up?

_____

d What did English ships carry to India?

_____

e What did English ships bring back from India?

_____

f How much profit might a successful merchant make?

_____

g Ships going to India had to sail in which two oceans?

_____

h Name two places where the East India Company had trading stations.

_____

B Colonies in America

A Puritan settler in America

The Spanish were the first to explore America. It was not long, though, before the English followed. Some went as pirates, and some as traders. But some set out to found **colonies**. (A colony is a group of people who make new lives in a far-off part of the world.)

Rich men **invested** in colonies. They put up money for the ships and supplies. They hoped to make profits from the clothes, nails, guns, etc. which they would ship to America for the settlers to buy. And more profits would come from the goods the settlers sent home for sale.

The settlers risked shipwreck, disease, famine, and attacks by the native people whose land they were taking. But land was cheap in the colonies, or even free, so most settlers soon had farms of their own. Some people hoped to find gold or adventure. Many Puritans went to America for freedom to worship as they wished. But some settlers had no choice – seven years' hard labour in the colonies was the punishment for quite small crimes.

The first English colony was founded in **Virginia** in 1607. (Look at the Map.) The first Puritans came to **New England**, further north, soon after. As more settlers arrived the colonies spread and new ones were started. In 1664 the English took over a

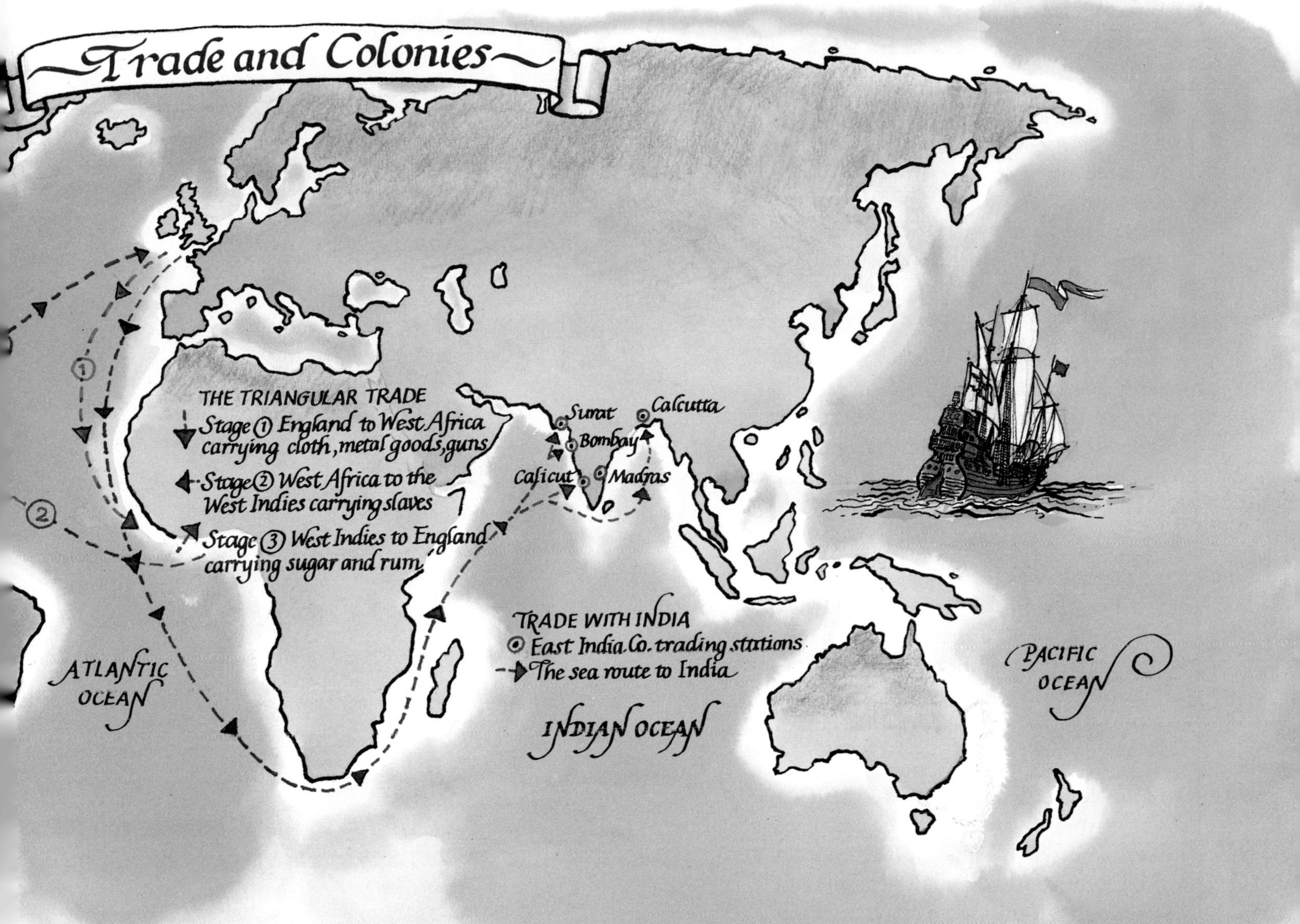

Trade and Colonies

THE TRIANGULAR TRADE
- Stage ① England to West Africa carrying cloth, metal goods, guns
- Stage ② West Africa to the West Indies carrying slaves
- Stage ③ West Indies to England carrying sugar and rum

ATLANTIC OCEAN

TRADE WITH INDIA
- ⊙ East India. Co. trading stations
- ⇢ The sea route to India

Surat Calcutta
Bombay
Calicut Madras

INDIAN OCEAN

PACIFIC OCEAN

Dutch colony and named it **New York**. By 1750, the British controlled most of North America's east coast.

In New England and New York, the settlers were farmers and fishermen. In Virginia, they learned to grow **tobacco**. (Smoking was a new habit in Europe, and tobacco was much in demand.) Rich 'planters' came over from England and bought up big estates. Convicts and, after 1700, black slaves, worked the land for them. The planters made fortunes. So did the merchants of Bristol and Glasgow who shipped and cured the tobacco.

Now try Exercise 14.2.

Exercise 14.2

Read **Section B**.
What were the **motives** of **i** the men who invested in colonies, and **ii** the settlers who went to live in the colonies? Read the list of suggestions below, then make two lists of motives – investors and settlers.

a To help poor people find a better life.
b To find gold and make their fortunes.
c To make money by selling things to the settlers.
d To find a place where they did not have to work hard for a living.
e To set up their own farms.
f To make money by selling what the settlers produced (e.g. tobacco).
g To find a more healthy place to live.
h To be able to worship in their own way.
i To do something different and exciting.

C Sugar and slaves

Silk, cotton, and tobacco were important for the growth of English trade, but not as important as **sugar**. Between 1600 and 1750 people began to eat much more sugar with their food. The sugar came from the West Indies, where the cane grew in 'plantations'. (Look at the Map on pages 70–71.)

Ships laden with sugar (and rum) sailed from Barbados to Bristol and Liverpool. Factories there refined it (made it pure). Then it was sold to merchants in English towns and cities, or abroad.

The owners of the plantations were rich English landlords. Many of them stayed at home, and lived on their profits. They had agents in the islands to manage their estates. The hard work of cutting and carting the cane and milling the sugar was done by black slaves.

The slaves came from West Africa. A lot of them were prisoners, captured in wars between tribes. Their captors sold them to white slave-traders, or exchanged them for cloth, metal goods, or guns from Europe. The traders branded them with their marks, and packed them into ships. The voyage to the West Indies took about eight weeks. A quarter of the slaves died at sea.

The slaves were sold in the West Indies to the planters' agents. There was always a brisk trade, for slaves lasted only a few years in the cane fields. Meanwhile, the ships were loaded with sugar and rum, and set sail for home. (Look at the Map again.) The trade made the merchants and planters rich. Most of them never saw the inside of a slave ship.

Now try Exercise 14.3.

Source  14a

A slave being branded

Source 14b

We brand the slaves on the chest with a hot iron. We do it so that we will know which ones are ours. It may seem cruel, but we try not to burn them too hard. We pack them on board – often six or seven hundred on a ship. The captains do it very cleverly, and much better than the French and English. Their slave ships are foul and stinking, but ours are clean and neat.

Written by a Dutch slave trader in West Africa in 1705.

Exercise 14.3

Look at **Source 14a** and read **Source 14b**.
Write notes on the sources:

a Who can you see in **Source 14a**?
b What examples of cruelty to slaves are mentioned in **Source 14b**?
c What excuses does the author of **Source 14b** give for the slave-traders' cruelty?

15 Daily Life

How a family lived depended on **who** they were. The courtiers set the fashions in clothes, food, and homes. The gentry and rich merchants copied what they could afford. The farmers and craftsmen came next, and last came the labouring poor. Fashion, of course, meant nothing to the poor – their concern was just to stay alive. (See Chapter 16.)

Source 15a

First course: A boiled pike or a stewed carp. A boiled pudding. A chine of veal and a chine of mutton. A calf's head pie. A roasted leg of mutton. A couple of large chickens, or a pig, or a piece of roast beef. A salad.

Second course: A dish of fat roasted chickens. A cold venison pasty. A dish of fried pasties. A fresh salmon. A couple of lobsters. A dish of tarts. A gammon of bacon. After this, serve cheese and fruit.

From a book of recipes written by Hannah Woolley in 1684.

A Food

In the time of the Tudors, most English people ate only two meals a day. They had dinner between eleven in the morning and twelve noon, and supper between five and eight o'clock in the evening. By 1750, nobles and gentry were dining at between two and three in the afternoon. To keep them going until then, they ate **breakfast** (tea and bread and butter) in the morning.

The nobles ate a great deal of meat. As well as beef, mutton, and pork, they were fond of rabbits, deer, and swans. And those who could afford it had sauces made from spices and herbs to go with the meat. They were fond of fish and shell-fish as well, and liked lots of tarts and puddings. But they were not so keen on vegetables.

In the sixteenth century, the law **forced** people to eat fish on two days each week. The reason was to strengthen the navy! By making people eat fish, the king made sure that there would be plenty of fishermen. And in time of war the fishermen were the crews of the ships in the navy.

A rich man's banquet consisted of three or more 'courses'. And a course meant a table filled with dishes. (See **Source 15a**.) At the end of the meal, what was left was taken out for the servants. What they did not eat was given to the poor.

Now try Exercise 15.1.

Source  15b

> *For broths of sundry tastes and sort,*
> *For beef, veal, mutton, lamb, and pork,*
> *Green sauce with calf's head and bacon,*
> *Pig and goose, and crammed-up capon,*
>
> *For pasties raised stiff with curious art,*
> *Pie, custard, florentine, and tart...*
> *Thanks be given for flesh and fishes,*
> *With this choice of tempting dishes.*

From a made-up story told in a long poem written by Thomas Dekker in 1612.

Exercise 15.1

Read **Section A** and **Sources 15a** and **15b**.
Put the correct halves of the sentences together, and write out the complete sentences.

a Source 15a was written...
b Source 15b was written...
c Source 15b is part of a longer poem and is...
d Source 15a is...
e Both sources tell us that well-off people ate a lot of...
f The sources show that people were not so keen on...
g The fiction source tells us the same kind of thing...

- vegetables and salads.
- a made-up story, or fiction.
- as the fact source about seventeenth-century food.
- by Thomas Dekker in 1612.
- from a real recipe book and is fact.
- by Hannah Woolley in 1684.
- meat, pies, pasties, and tarts.

B Clothes

Tudor courtiers were great show-offs, above all in their dress. Men and women liked fine materials and bright colours. They were fond of gold and silver thread stitched into fancy patterns. Both sexes wore garments edged with lace or fur. Everyone had lots of rings and bracelets.

Ladies' gowns had full skirts, slashed open at the front to reveal **farthingales** (hooped petticoats in fine lace). The men wore **doublets** (long tunics) and hose. Both men and women wore starched lace ruffs round their necks. (See **Source 15c**.)

After 1600, all men began wearing breeches instead of doublet and hose. At the time of the Civil War, how they dressed depended on which side they took. Roundheads wore plain, dark clothes. Cavaliers dressed brightly, with lots of lace and ribbon. Under the Commonwealth, England's rulers all dressed in Roundhead style. When Charles II was restored, the bright colours and ribbons made a come-back.

By the 1690s, ladies' gowns had full skirts, tight bodices, and low necklines. Ladies wore lots of make-up – paint, rouge, and beauty patches. Wigs, with long, curly ringlets (called 'periwigs') were the fashion for men. They were so heavy and hot that most men shaved their heads.

Now try Exercise 15.2.

Sir Thomas More and
family in the
sixteenth century

Lord Buckingham and
family in the
seventeenth century

The Shudi family in
the eighteenth
century

Ordinary people's clothing in the eighteenth century

C Education

Children were not forced by law to go to school in Tudor and Stuart times. If they did attend, in most cases, the parents had to pay fees. In spite of this, by 1700 most children in towns got some schooling.

The sons and daughters of great lords had private tutors. As part of their studies, the sons spent from three to five years with their tutors on a 'Grand Tour' abroad. They learned to speak French, looked at works of art and buildings, and studied the laws of the countries of Europe.

The gentry and merchants sent their sons to the **grammar schools**. This is where they learned to read, write, and speak **Latin**. Latin was still the language of scholars in the universities. And it was to Oxford or Cambridge that the young gentry went after grammar school. After that, they stud-

ied the law for a few years at the **Inns of Court** in London.

Girls were expected to marry at an early age. So the daughters of the gentry stayed at home. They were taught to read and write, and to sew and manage a home by their mothers. Neither their fathers nor their mothers wanted to waste money on education.

Parish schools and, by 1700, charity schools were for the sons and daughters of craftsmen and labourers. They were better than nothing, but only just. The children learned to read and write, and to do simple sums. A lot of time was spent on scripture. But the teachers were untrained and badly paid, and there were not many books or much equipment. As a rule, the pupils left school to start work when they were ten or eleven years old.

Now try Exercise 15.3.

Village schools in the sixteenth and eighteenth centuries

Source  15f

I could read when I was four years old. By the time I was seven, my father employed eight tutors – for languages, music, dancing, writing, and needlework. Father started me on Latin, and I made good progress. I was soon ahead of my brothers, even though my Latin tutor was a dull fellow.

I always liked my books best. My mother said that all the reading and study would harm my health. And she was not pleased when I would not practise my music and dancing. As for needlework, I hated it.

Written by Mrs. Lucy Hutchinson in about 1657.

Exercise 15.3

Read **Section C** and **Source 15f**. Answer the questions in sentences.

a Which **facts** can you find in **Source 15f**? (Write down four facts.)
b What was Lucy proud of?
c What did Lucy dislike?
d What did Lucy's father think about education for girls?
e What did Lucy's mother think about her daughter's education?
f What did Lucy think of her Latin tutor?

D Health

Between 1650 and 1750, more people moved to the towns, and the nation's health got worse. All towns were unhealthy – none of them had proper sewers or pure drinking water. Over-crowding helped disease to spread. And after 1700 cheap **gin** ruined the health of the poor.

Disease led quickly to death. A lot of children died young, and many women died in childbirth. People were saddened, but not surprised, by the sudden loss of a loved one. Most of them said that it was God's will that the person should die – there was nothing that they could do about it.

Only those who could pay the fees could call in doctors. This was not such a bad thing for the poor, for doctors were not much use. They helped by giving good advice, such as not to eat or drink too much. But they also did harm – they still **bled** patients suffering from fever.

Each family had its recipes for cures, kept with the recipes for pickles and jam. Some contained good sense, but many were useless or worse. For example, 'to cure baldness, rub your head with garlic and wash it in vinegar.' In every market-place there was a man selling 'miracle' cures, and plenty of foolish buyers.

In one sense, though, the nation's health improved. The changes in farming (see Chapter 1) meant that there was more **fresh** meat – at least for those who could afford it.

Now try Exercises 15.4 and 15.5.

Source **15g**

A brass memorial in Durnford Church, Wiltshire. The inscription says:
Here lyeth the body of Edward Young of Little Dorneford Esq:, sonne & heyre (son & heir) of John Young Esq: & of Mary his wife, one of ye fower (four) daughters & Coheyres (co-heirs) of Thom. Trapnell of Mounceton Farley, Esq:. Which Edw: (This man Edward Younge) married Joan, ye eldest daughter of Laurence Hide of West Hatche, Esq: & had by her 6 sones & 8 daughters, who dyed (i.e. Edward Younge died) Febr: 18, 1607.

Hear ye! Hear ye! New Miracle Cure for baldness, foot and mouth, tooth- ache and acne. Just add goat's milk.

Exercise 15.4

Read **Section D**.
Copy the sentences and write TRUE or FALSE after each one.

a Towns were healthier than the countryside. _____

b Gin was cheap between 1700 and 1750, so many poor people drank too much and ruined their health. _____

c Families were large, but many children died young. _____

d Sudden death was a common event and did not surprise people. _____

e Most doctors were glad to work among the poor without payment. _____

f Families kept their own lists of remedies and cures. _____

g No one was fooled by sellers of 'quack' medicines. _____

Exercise 15.5

Study **Source 15g**.

a Make your own notes, answering these questions:
   i What does **Source 15g** tell us about Edward Young and his family?
   ii What makes you think that Edward Young was a rich man?
   iii Did all families put up brass plates in churches? If not, why not?
   iv Are church brasses a useful type of source? What do they tell us? What do they not tell us?

b Discuss your answers to the questions with other pupils in a group.

c Make a group tape, or give brief talks to the rest of the class, giving your group's answers.

16 The Poor

A Living conditions of the poor

About half the people in England were poor. They seldom had enough to eat, and sometimes starved. Their clothes were second-hand, and a lot of poor children had no shoes. In the villages, their homes were simple shacks, with clay or wooden walls, thatched roofs, and no glass in the windows. They had no chimneys, just a hole in the roof. A chest, a bench, and a trestle table would be their only furniture.

The poor in the countryside were farm labourers and their families. The men's wages were low, and their wives helped out by making cheese and spinning wool. As soon as they were able, children had to work. The girls helped their mothers at home, and the boys earned a few pence minding sheep or scaring birds from the fields.

Even so, farm workers were well off in some respects. They had gardens, where they grew cabbages, peas, and beans. And they could keep a cow and some sheep on the common. So they had butter, cheese and wool to sell. They needed the money to pay the rent and buy their bread.

But when common land was enclosed (see Chapter 1), the poor suffered. The land was carved up into fields, and there was nowhere for their animals to graze. As a result, they had nothing to sell, and became even poorer.

Labourers in towns had to buy all their food. Their wages were poor, if they could get jobs at all. They lived in crowded, dirty hovels. In parts of London the poor were crammed fifteen or twenty to a room. And there were some with no homes at all.

Now try Exercise 16.1.

A farm labourer's cottage

Source  16a

Only rich men can afford to eat a joint of fresh meat once a month. The poor have to sell their young pigs and chickens to pay the rent. They cannot afford to eat the eggs their hens lay, and they must sell the best of their butter and cheese. They make do with skimmed milk and curds.

Written by Richard Baxter in 1691.

Source 16b

Half the people in England eat meat every day. A quarter eat meat twice a week. The rest, who are the poor, have meat only once a week.

Written by Gregory King in 1696.

'Beer Street' in London – a drawing by the eighteenth-century artist, William Hogarth. He shows us what the London streets looked like, and warns us that he thought the problems of the poor were caused by too much drink.

Exercise 16.1

Read **Section A**, and **Sources 16a** and **16b**.

a Write out these sentences, and write TRUE or FALSE after each of them.
  i **Sources 16a** and **16b** were written in the same century.
  ii **Sources 16a** and **16b** were written by the same person.
  iii Both sources say that the rich ate a lot of meat.
  iv **Source 16b** says that even the poor ate meat once a week.
  v **Source 16a** says that the poor could not afford to eat fresh meat.
  vi **Source 16a** explains why poor people could not afford fresh meat.
b Can you think of any possible reasons why **Sources 16a** and **16b** say different things about poor people's food? (Write a short paragraph.)

BEER STREET.

*Beer, happy Produce of our Isle
Can sinewy strength impart,
And wearied with Fatigue and Toil
Can cheer each manly Heart.*

*Labour and Art upheld by Thee
Successfully advance,
We quaff Thy balmy Juice with Glee
And Water leave to France.*

*Genius of Health, thy grateful Taste
Rivals the Cup of Jove,
And warns each English generous Breast
With Liberty and Love.*

B Prices and wages

England's population increased from just over two million in 1500 to five million in 1650. (Look at Graph A.) The farmers grew more wheat, rye, and barley, but not as much as the people needed. So there was a shortage of bread, and the price rose. All the other prices followed.

Graph B shows how prices rose. It tells you that a 'basket' with so much bread, a piece of cloth, a pair of shoes, some candles, and a few other items would have cost £1 in 1505. It says that to buy exactly the same 'basket' of goods you would have had to pay £6.82 in 1645.

Wages also rose, but they did not go up as much as prices. Poor peasants, who could not afford to buy bread for their children, left their villages. They drifted to the towns, but soon found that life there was worse than in the villages they had left. In every town, gangs of men, women, and children begged in the streets.

Things got slightly better after 1650, when prices stopped rising. After 1700 they even fell a little. Wages did not fall, so men who were in work were better off. But the numbers of the poor did not fall much. And when there was a bad harvest, the price of bread shot up again.

Now try Exercise 16.2.

Exercise 16.2

Study **Graph A** and **Graph B**. Copy the questions and fill in the spaces as you go.

a What was England's population in 1500? _____

b What was the population in 1600? _____

c By how much did the population increase between 1600 and 1700? _____

d There were two periods when the population was not increasing. Which was the longer of these periods? From _____ to _____

e What did the 'basket' of goods cost in 1505? _____

f When did the cost of the 'basket' reach £2. About _____

g What did the 'basket' cost in 1600? _____

h By how much did the cost of the 'basket' fall between 1645 and 1685? About _____ pence.

i What did the 'basket' cost in 1745? _____

j Why did prices rise when the population was rising? (See paragraph 1 of **Section B**.)

_____

Graph A: The population of England, 1500–1750

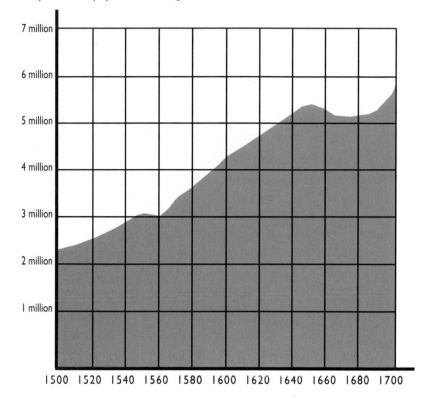

Graph B: Prices 1505–1745

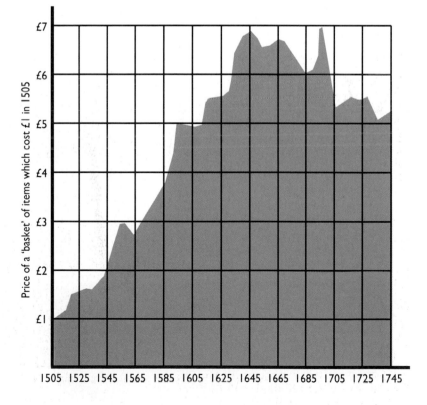

Price of a 'basket' of items which cost £1 in 1505

C **The poor law**

In the sixteenth century, there was no unemployment pay and no child benefit. There were no old age pensions and no National Health Service. Instead, each town had 'almshouses' and 'hospitals' to look after the old and sick. Rich merchants often left money to almshouses in their wills.

After 1550 there were so many poor that the almshouses could not cope. The bands of beggars worried the Government. It got Parliament to pass laws, partly to help the poor, and partly to force them to work.

The new laws said that those who could afford it should pay a tax to help the 'deserving poor'. This meant the old, the disabled, and the sick who could not work. But the Government said that healthy young men and women who had no jobs must be lazy. It called them 'vagabonds', and said that they had to be punished. Some were whipped, some were branded with red-hot irons, and some were put in the stocks.

People agreed that the poor could not be left to starve. But no-one liked paying taxes to help care for them. In the eighteenth century, some parishes built 'workhouses'. These were homes and work-places for the poor. To scare off the 'scroungers', they made the workhouses as unpleasant as they could.

Now try Exercises 16.3, 16.4 and 16.5.

Exercise 16.3

Read **Section C**.
Draw a time-line from 1450 to 1750. Mark the fifteenth, sixteenth, seventeenth, and eighteenth centuries. Write these sentences in the correct places on the time-line.

a In 1723 Parliament allowed parishes to combine to build workhouses.
b A law passed in 1572 said that all who could afford it had to pay a local tax to help the poor.
c In 1662 magistrates got the power to send strangers back to their own parishes if they looked as if they would need poor relief.
d An act passed in 1536 said that each parish had to have a fund of money to help to look after the poor.
e A law passed in 1597 ordered parishes to find work for the unemployed.
f In 1496 sheriffs and mayors were ordered to put vagabonds in the stocks for three days and nights.

Source  16c

A vagabond is whipped through the streets

Science and Superstition

A Observation and experiment

The most important change that took place between 1600 and 1750 was the start of modern **science**. Before 1600, science was something you read in books. And the books had been written by **ancient Greeks**. After 1600, scientists began to believe what they saw with their own eyes.

In the Middle Ages, science and magic were not far apart. **Alchemists** tried to turn lead into gold. **Astrologers** told the future by looking at the stars. After the end of the Middle Ages (about the year 1500), there was still a lot of **superstition**. In 1700, educated men still believed in lucky charms. And most common folk were still scared of witches.

Science began to change soon after 1600. **Sir Francis Bacon** said that a scientist's first task was **observation**. Bacon meant that he should look at things and describe what he saw (not what the books said he should see). In some cases, he had to do **experiments**, and write down the results.

To work this way, scientists needed new instruments. Between 1600 and 1750, they invented a lot of things that

Science in the sixteenth century – An alchemist's laboratory

Source 16d

A gentleman and a beggar

Source 16e

Labourers' children have to be kept by the parish. The more children a poor man has, the more money he gets from the parish. The allowance is paid to the father. He often spends it in the public house, and his children do not get enough to eat.

Written by John Locke in the 1690s.

Exercise 16.4

Study **Sources 16c**, and **16d**.
Write a short essay, with the title 'How the artists saw the beggars'.
Use these notes as a guide:

a Describe what you can see in the pictures. – How are the beggars dressed? What are they doing, or what is happening to them?
b What do you think the artists thought about the beggars? Were they sorry for them? Did they think the beggars were layabouts? Did both the artists think the same?

Exercise 16.5

Read **Sources 16e**, **16f**, and **16g**.
Then answer the questions in sentences.

a These sources tell us what some people thought about the poor in the seventeenth and eighteenth centuries. Are they primary or secondary sources?
b What does John Locke (**Source 16e**) say that makes you think that he had a low opinion of labouring men?
c Robert Nelson (**Source 16f**) thought that the poor were lucky. How many reasons did he give for this opinion?
d Do you think that Robert Nelson was a poor man? If he had been poor, would he have agreed that he was lucky?
e Soame Jenyns (**Source 16g**) thought that poverty was necessary. How many reasons did he give for his opinion?
f Do you think that Soame Jenyns was poor? (Give your reasons.)
g Why do you think that there are not many sources giving **poor people's** opinions?

Source 16f

The poor are lucky – they have a more godly life than the rich. They have no luxuries, and luxury just makes men proud. They have to work hard, so they are not tempted to be lazy. They can not afford to eat and drink too much, so they are healthy in body and mind. They know what it is like to go hungry, so they are kind to neighbours who fall on hard times. And they get very little happiness on earth, so they think a lot about Heaven.

Written by Robert Nelson in 1715.

Source 16g

There has to be poverty. If there were no poor, who would take orders from the rich? Who would do the humble and dirty jobs? Who would work the land? Who would do the tradesmen's labouring jobs? Without the poor, we should all go short, instead of just a few starving now and then.

Written by Soame Jenyns in 1761.

we now take for granted. First was the **telescope**, to look at the stars and the planets. Next came the **microscope**, to look at things too small for the human eye. Then, after long research, they made a **thermometer** that really worked.

All the leading men of the time became keen on science. In London, Thomas Gresham founded a college, which took his name. Its members met each week to listen to lectures and hear the latest news. In 1662, King Charles II gave the college his support, and it became the **Royal Society**. All the top scientists belonged to it, as they still do today.

Now try Exercises 17.1 and 17.2.

Source 17a

> **20th January 1665. Mr. Batten tells me that he has never had colic pain since he started to carry a hare's foot about with him. I bought a hare today and took it home. As soon as I touched its foot my pain went away.**
> **26th March 1665. I have never had the colic pain since I started wearing the hare's foot. On the other hand, it may be the turpentine pill I take each morning. Or it may be the two together.**

From Samuel Pepys's diary. Pepys went to Cambridge University, and became a Fellow of the Royal Society. He was one of the best-educated men of his day.

Exercise 17.1

Read **Section A**. Then write sentences to show that you know what these words mean.

scientists alchemist astrologer superstition observation experiment telescope microscope thermometer Royal Society

Exercise 17.2

Read **Source 17a**, and look again at what **Section A** says about superstition. Make your own notes to answer these questions:

a Is **Source 17a** a primary source?
b Who was the author of **Source 17a**? What do we know about him?
c What does **Source 17a** say to make us think that educated people in the 1660s were superstitious?
d Scientists are supposed to make up their minds after **observing** the facts. Which facts did Pepys observe? Did he make up his mind about the hare's foot?
e Most people were far less educated than Pepys. How superstitious do you think they were?

B Some great scientists

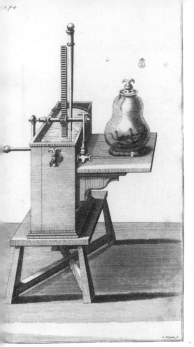

Boyle's air pump, which he used to make a vacuum

William Harvey demonstrating his ideas to Charles I

Robert Boyle was one man who took Bacon's advice to observe and record. In his laboratory in Oxford he did hundreds of experiments. He invented an air-pump, to pump air out of a vessel, and so make a **vacuum**. This made him think that air could be weighed. He went on to attack the Greek idea that there were just four **elements** – earth, water, air, and fire. In his day, men said he was wrong, but we know he was right.

Thanks to **William Harvey**, the science of **medicine** made a big leap forward. In a book which he wrote in 1628, Harvey said that blood moved round the body. He said that it flowed out from the heart through the arteries, and back through the veins. This was the idea of the **circulation of the blood**. Like Boyle, Harvey was not believed at first.

Sir Isaac Newton was the greatest scientist of his age. He was **not** the first man to say that the earth revolved round the sun. And he did **not** discover gravity. But he worked out laws to show how these things happened. And he showed that **mathematics** was at the heart of all **physics**. The men and women of his time did recognize Newton as a great man. His work made them think that science would soon solve all problems.

Now try Exercises 17.3 and 17.4.

Sir Isaac Newton as shown on a 1980s pound note

Exercise 17.3

Read **Section B**. Copy the questions and fill in the spaces using words from the list below.

telescope mathematics circulation veins Oxford sun space air-pump gravity Cambridge medicine chemistry fire moon arteries physics

a Where was Robert Boyle's laboratory?

_____

b What did Boyle invent to make a vacuum?

_____

c The ancient Greeks believed in four elements, which were water, earth, air, and what? _____

d Harvey did a great deal for which branch of science?

_____

e Which word used by Harvey means that the blood goes round and round the body? _____

f Harvey said that the blood flows out from the heart through what? _____

g Newton knew that the earth revolved around what?

_____

h Newton knew that what caused objects to fall?

_____

i Newton showed that you could use what to explain the laws of physics? _____

Source  17b

I began to think that the blood must go round in a circle. Later, I proved that it is true. I saw that the blood is driven out of the heart, through the arteries, into the lungs and other parts of the body. It returns through the veins to the heart. So it goes on in an endless motion, with the heart acting as a pump.

Written by William Harvey in 1628.

The Royal Observatory at Greenwich

Source 17c

I have heard Harvey say that when his book on the circulation of the blood came out he lost a lot of patients. The public thought that he was crack-brained. All the doctors were against him. Many of them wrote books attacking him. But 20 or 30 years later, all the world's universities thought that he was right. Soon, everyone else thought the same.

Written by John Aubrey, who lived from 1626 to 1697.

Exercise 17.4

Read **Sources 17b** and **17c**. Then write two paragraphs in your own words:

a What were Harvey's ideas about these things?
  i How the blood moves round the body,
  ii What the arteries do,
  iii What the veins do,
  iv What the heart does.
b What did Harvey's patients, the public, and other doctors think about Harvey's theory,
  i at first, and
  ii twenty to thirty years later?

C Witches

Witches being hanged

Most men and women knew nothing of science. To them, the world was full of spirits and **witches**. Witches (nearly always women) were supposed to have sold their souls to the devil. In return, he had given them magic powers. They could cast spells and give people the 'evil eye'. If they did so, their victims would be taken ill, or die, or be hit by bad luck.

Witches, so they said, lived alone, apart from a spirit that helped them in their work. This often took the form of a pet, such as a cat. So village people kept clear of old women who lived alone with their cats. They hung horseshoes and bunches of herbs over their own cottage doors to protect them from the witches' powers.

Not only the ignorant and poor believed in witches. In 1542, the gentry, merchants, and lords in Parliament made witchcraft a crime. The law stayed in force until 1736. In that time, a few hundred women, most of them old, were hanged. (Witches were not burned in England.)

A simple chain of events could bring a 'witch' to trial. An old woman would come begging at a farmhouse door. The busy farmer's wife would send her off with nothing. Shortly after, the farmer would fall ill and die. His wife would remember the old woman, and accuse her of being a witch. The old woman would be arrested and tortured. Under torture, she would 'confess' that she was a witch.

In the late seventeenth century, educated people stopped believing in witches. Poor old women were still brought to court, but judges refused to find them guilty. The last hanging for witchcraft in England took place at Exeter in 1685. The common folk, of course, went on believing in witches many years after witchcraft ceased to be a crime.

Now try Exercise 17.5.

Source 17d

David Seaton had a maid called Jill Duncan. This Jill often helped the sick, and many of her cures were so quick that they looked like miracles. Her master was surprised by her skill. Then he became suspicious. He began to think that Jill might be a witch.

When David asked Jill how she did these things, she made no answer. So he tried torture to make her talk. He crushed her fingers, then bound her head tightly with a rope. In the end, she confessed that she was a witch. She said that she worked with the devil, and that she was planning to make the king ill with her magic.

From a report of a witch trial in Scotland in 1591.

Exercise 17.5

Read **Section C** and **Source 17d**. Discuss the questions in a group. Then do one of these: **i** Write down your answers, **ii** Make a group tape.

a Which things in **Source 17d** are probably true?

b Which things in **Source 17d** could not be true?

c What makes you think that David Seaton believed in witchcraft?

d Do you think that Jill Duncan believed in witchcraft?

e Do you think that, in the end, Jill believed that she was a witch?

f Does the author of **Source 17d** say whether he believed in witches? Do you think that he believed in witches?

18 Architecture, Art and the Theatre

Source 18a

Source 18b

Two views of Chipchase Castle in Northumberland, close to the Scottish border. **Source 18a** shows the part built in the fourteenth century, when there were regular border wars. **Source 18b** shows the part built in 1621, when there was peace on the border.

A Country houses

You can read the history of England in the buildings of the past. In the Middle Ages, a great deal of the nation's wealth was in the hands of the Church. The finest buildings at the time were the **cathedrals** and **abbeys**. Also, the kings and lords were often at war, so they built massive **castles**, with high, thick walls and small windows.

After the **Reformation**, in the time of the Tudors, the Church lost a lot of its wealth. Its land passed into the hands of the gentry and nobles. Now they were the ones who built in style. Also, apart from the 1640s, civil wars came to an end. Peace came even to the borders of Scotland and Wales. So the gentry and lords built **country houses**, not castles.

Houses varied in size, depending on how rich the owners were. But most of them had big windows, grand doorways, and high, stylish chimneys. At first, the great hall was the main room in the house. Later, separate dining rooms and drawing rooms were built. Upstairs, most of them had a **long gallery**, where the lord and lady took exercise in bad weather.

The main rooms in the best houses had ornate plaster ceilings, and chimney pieces in carved wood or stone. Tapestries or oak panelling covered the walls. Later, the fashion changed to hanging paintings on the walls. Often,

Source  **18c**

Burghley House. A country house built in the reign of Queen Elizabeth I.

Source  **18d**

Belton House in Lincolnshire, built in the eighteenth century

these were portraits of the lord and his family.

Buildings tell the story of the growth of **trade** as well. (See Chapter 14.) Merchants, as they grew richer, built bigger, finer houses in the towns. Then many of them bought land, built country houses, and moved out to their new estates.

Now try Exercises 18.1 and 18.2.

Source 18e

A rich merchant's house in Coggeshall

Exercise 18.1

Read **Section A**, and look at **Sources 18a**, **18b**, **18c**, **18d**, and **18e**.

a How did the nobles, gentry, and merchants become rich enough to build fine country houses? Why did they build houses, and not castles?
Copy the chart below and fill in the spaces.

Cause	Result
1. _____ _____ _____	Nobles and gentry got land that had belonged to the Church. They became richer, and built country houses.
2. No more civil wars (apart from the 1640s) in England. Peace also on the Scottish and Welsh borders.	_____ _____ _____
3. Trade grew, so merchants became richer.	i _____ _____ ii _____ _____

b Draw a picture of a country house.

Source 18f

A sixteenth-century room with furniture at Moseley Old Hall, Staffordshire

Source  18g

An eighteenth-century room with furniture at Saltram in Devon

Source 18h

Anne of Cleves (Henry VIII's fourth wife) by Hans Holbein

B Painting and sculpture

Artists in the Middle Ages worked for the Church. They painted pictures of Jesus and the saints on canvas, or wood, or on church walls. Then, between 1400 and 1500, there came a change. Artists in Italy began painting **portraits** of the people of their time. Their subjects, of course, were the rich – lords and ladies, merchants and their wives.

The new fashion spread to the rest of Europe. Painters from Italy and Germany came to England to paint Henry VIII and his wives. Nobles and gentry copied the king. They too wanted to see themselves and their families on canvas.

All the best painters came from abroad, though. There were not many great English portrait painters before the year 1700. What the English were good at was **miniatures**. These were small portraits that men and women hung in lockets around their necks.

Sculptors, like painters, had worked mainly for the Church. But at the Reformation, stone carvings of saints were removed. In the 1640s and 1650s, the Puritans, who hated ornaments in churches, destroyed still more. But sculpture made a come-back. By 1750 the lords and gentry were filling their houses and gardens with sculptures, most of them from abroad.

Now try Exercise 18.3

Source 18i

A miniature of Sir Walter Raleigh by Nicholas Hilliard

 Source 18j

Source 18k

Above right: A formal garden, with its gravel paths, small flower beds, and clipped shrubs, all in regular patterns. Formal gardens were the fashion in the sixteenth and seventeenth centuries.

Above left: An eighteenth-century *landscaped garden* (at Stourhead in Wiltshire). Here, the trees and plants grew in a much more natural way.

Exercise 18.3

Read **Section B**, and look at **Sources 18h, 18i, 18j,** and **18k**. Then write sentences to show that you know what each of these words and phrases mean:

portrait miniature sculpture formal garden landscaped garden

Source **18l**

C The theatre

The Swan Theatre in London in 1596

People in Tudor times made their own amusements, such as music and dancing. But it was a special treat to see a **play**. This was very rare, for outside London there were no theatres. Once in a while, though, a band of **travelling players** arrived in a town and put on a show.

In the 1570s, the first theatres were opened in London. They looked just like inn yards. (Look at **Source 18l**.) Some of the spectators sat in the **galleries** round the sides, overlooking the stage. Rich lords sat on the edge of the stage, and sometimes joined in the play. The 'groundlings' – the poorer folk – stood in the **pit**.

In many ways, the theatres were different from those of today. There were no lights, so the plays were staged in daylight. There were no curtains, and there was very little scenery. The actors wore normal clothes, not special costumes, and **boys** took all the women's parts.

The greatest of the playwrights was **William Shakespeare**. As a young man, he came down to London from Stratford-upon-Avon. He joined a group of actors, started writing plays, and became famous. After his death his plays (more than thirty of them) were printed. They have been read ever since, and acted in theatres all over the world.

Puritans did not like the theatres. When they were in power, in the 1640s, they closed the theatres down. When Charles II was restored, though, they were opened up again. There were some changes – now the theatres had roofs, lights (candles), and curtains. Also, for the first time in England, women took part in the plays.

Now try Exercises 18.4 and 18.5.

Source **18m**

Rich young men with nothing to do are always at the theatre. That's where they mix with the tramps, thieves, and tricksters who meet there to plot their crimes. And the plays they see are full of wickedness and cheating. Those who watch are soon persuaded to copy what they see.

Apprentices and servants waste their time at the theatre, neglecting their work. People who should know better go there instead of to church. On top of all that, theatres can make you ill – it's easy to catch an infection in the crowd.

Letter written by a Puritan Lord Mayor of London in 1597.

Source **18n**

Going to the theatre does young people no harm. If they don't go they might get up to worse mischief elsewhere. Most of the plays set a good example – they tell about the brave actions of the men of the past. And if you do see cheats and liars on the stage, they always come to a bad end.

Written in 1592 by Thomas Nashe, a writer who hated Puritans.

Exercise 18.4

Look at **Source 18l**, read **Sources 18m** and **18n**, and read **Section C**. Plan and write an essay with the title: 'The theatre in the time of Elizabeth I'. Include paragraphs on:

  i What the theatre looked like.
 ii The sort of people who went to the theatre.
iii The sort of plays they saw there.
 iv Different opinions about the theatre – who was against the theatre, who was in favour of it, and their reasons.

Exercise 18.5

Look at the cartoons and read the notes about Shakespeare's plays. Write out the sentences below. After each sentence, write either TRUE or FALSE.

a Everything in Shakespeare's history plays is true. _____
b Shakespeare sometimes borrowed stories from other authors. _____
c Henry V and Julius Caesar were real people. _____
d *Macbeth* was a tragedy. _____
e The story in *Romeo and Juliet* was true. _____
f *Romeo and Juliet* has a happy ending. _____
g The story in *A Midsummer Night's Dream* is fiction. _____
h Shakespeare made up the story of *The Comedy of Errors* himself. _____

William Shakespeare

William Shakespeare's Plays

Some of Shakespeare's plays were about real people who lived in the past. Shakespeare, of course, made up all of the speeches. But a lot of the facts in his <u>history</u> plays were true.

In other plays Shakespeare made up the whole story, or used a story which he knew was fiction. Some of the plays were <u>tragedies</u> (with sad endings). Others were <u>comedies</u> (with happy endings).

<u>Henry V</u> is about the great soldier-king and his wars in France. Most of the events really happened.

<u>Julius Caesar</u> tells the true story of murder and civil war in ancient Rome.

<u>Romeo and Juliet</u> were young lovers whose families were always at war. The made up story comes to a sad end.

The king of the fairies in <u>A Midsummer Night's Dream</u> quarrels with his wife. He makes her fall in love with a weaver called Bottom, and he gives Bottom an ass's head.

<u>Macbeth</u> is about a Scottish noble who killed the king and took his crown. Macbeth comes to a tragic end. Most of the story is fiction.

The story in <u>The Comedy of Errors</u> comes from an ancient Roman play. It is all about two sets of identical twins.

Cross references between exercises in this book and National Curriculum Programme of Study. (Bold references are especially relevant.)

Chapters	1	2	3	4	5	6	7	8	9	10	11	12	13	14	15	16	17	18

Chronological understanding

		1	2	3	4	5	6	7	8	9	10	11	12	13	14	15	16	17	18
a	Historical knowledge	1.1 1.3	2.1 2.4	3.4	4.2 4.3	5.1 5.2	6.1	7.1 7.4	8.2 8.5	9.1	10.1 10.4	11.2	12.1 12.5	13.1 13.2	14.1	15.2 15.4	16.2	17.3 17.4	18.1
b	Concepts and terminology		2.3	3.1					8.4		10.3	11.1						17.1	18.3
c	Chronology – dates and sequence			3.3	4.1	5.2											16.3		
d	Chronology – conventions	**1.4**						7.3									16.3		

Knowledge and understanding

		1	2	3	4	5	6	7	8	9	10	11	12	13	14	15	16	17	18
a	Cause and consequence		**2.4** **2.5**				6.3		8.2		10.5								18.1
b	Motivation							**7.5**		9.4				13.1	14.2				
c	Continuity and change							7.4				11.3		13.4		15.2	16.2	17.4	18.2
d	Different features of situations	1.5				5.5				9.3			12.3	13.3			16.5		18.4

Historical interpretation

		1	2	3	4	5	6	7	8	9	10	11	12	13	14	15	16	17	18
a	Distinguishing fact and fiction															15.1		17.5	18.5
b	Different versions of events and topics		2.2		4.5	5.3					10.1	11.5							
c	Recognizing fact and opinion			**3.5**						9.2			12.2			15.3	16.4		
d	Different interpretations			**3.2**			6.4	7.2	8.3	9.5			12.4	13.2			16.1		
e	Reasons for different interpretations									**9.6**			12.4	13.2			16.1		

Historical enquiry

		1	2	3	4	5	6	7	8	9	10	11	12	13	14	15	16	17	18
a	Acquiring information	1.3	2.1	3.4	4.2	5.1	6.1	7.1		9.1	10.4	11.2	12.1	13.4	14.1	15.4	16.2	17.3	18.5
b	Sources – authorship and dates	**1.2**	2.2						8.3			11.4				15.1			
c	Primary and secondary sources				**4.4**	5.3			8.3			11.4					16.5	17.2	
d	Making deductions from sources	1.5					6.5		8.1	9.3	10.2				14.3			17.2	
e	Using different kinds of source			3.5			6.2		8.5		10.1	11.4		13.5	14.3				18.4
f	Value and reliability of evidence				4.5	**5.4**								13.5		15.5			

Most of the exercises also seek to develop organisational and communication skills.